MW00528450
GARY LLOYD NOLAND
COLLECTED
CHAMBER WORKS
Volume 1
Music in Varying Combinations
for Violin, Viola, Cello & Piano
(inclusive of all instrumental parts)
7TH SPECIES PUBLICATIONS
13080 Princeton Court, Lake Oswego, OR 97035
email: nolandgary5@gmail.com
website: https://composergarynoland.godaddysites.com/

Published by 7th Species
13080 Princeton Court
Lake Oswego OR 97035

First Edition, First Printing of COLLECTED CHAMBER WORKS: Music in Varying Combinations for Piano & Strings, January, 2022.

Composer's website: https://composergarynoland.godaddysites.com/
Contact email: nolandgary5@gmail.com

ISBN/SKU: 978-1-7323023-7-2

First printed 2022

Title page and all interior illustrations by Lon Gaylord Dylan (the composer's visual artist alter ego).

Also by

GARY LLOYD NOLAND

Books

COLLECTED PIANO WORKS: Volume 1
COLLECTED PIANO WORKS: Volume 2
JAGDLIED: a Chamber Novel for Narrator, Musicians, Pantomimists, Dancers & Culinary Artists
NOTHING IS MORE: a High Black Comedy in Verse with Music for Six Actors

Music CDs

Available from NorthPacificMusic.com:

SELECTED MUSIC FROM VENGE ART
ROYAL OILWORKS MUSIC
24 INTERLUDES FOR PIANO OP. 71, VOL. 1
24 INTERLUDES FOR PIANO OP. 71, VOL. 2
24 POSTLUDES FOR PIANO OP. 72, VOL. 1
24 POSTLUDES FOR PIANO OP. 72, VOL. 2

in collaboration with other composers:

PASSION
PLAYERLESS PIANOS

Available from 7th Species at: https://composergarynoland.godaddysites.com/

20 COVIDITTIES OP. 116 (double CD)
ENTROPIC ABANDON (double CD)
MUSIC OF RAGE, SORROW, LOVE, LAUGHTER & BUREAUCRACY (double CD, release pending)
DISSONAPHOBIC FEVER DREAMS Op. 118
STATE-OF-THE-ART EAR EXERCISES FOR MUSICAL COGNOSCENTI Op. 119
WAYWARD AFFECTS & AFFLICTIONS Op. 120

Music Scores

Multiple scores available from 7th Species (Freeland) Publications, J.W. Pepper, Sheet Music Plus, RGM

Composer's Notes

WALTZ FANTASY for violin & piano Op. 87 (2007, revised 2009) received its world premiere by violinist Inés Voglar and pianist Jeff Payne (both members of Portland, Oregon's contemporary music ensemble fEARnoMUSIC) on the historic inaugural concert of Cascadia Composers (now the largest chapter of NACUSA and one of the leading composer organizations on the West Coast) at the Old Church in Portland, Oregon on March 9th, 2009. This concert was historic on account of its having been the critical catalyst that launched and sparked to life Portland's now famously vibrant contemporary classical music scene. Prior to the moment Cascadia Composers was officially established by its seven visionary founding members—composers David S. Bernstein (who deserves kudos as the originator of the group), Jack Gabel, Dan Senn, Greg Steinke, Tomas Svoboda, Jeff Winslow, and this author—Portland was a city whose right hand didn't know what its left hand was up to in terms of its (then) chaotic, disjointed, and incoherent contemporary classical music landscape. When Noland first moved to Portland in 2005, he remarked from the outset that it was exceedingly difficult to make head or tail of the contemporary music scene in both the city's urban core and its immediate environs. Composers in various communities of the Portland metro area and beyond were all but incognizant of the existence of their fellow travelers (not to mention their musical comings, goings, and doings) in other parts of the city. Moreover, Portland appeared to offer very few if any viable performance venues enabling its resident composers to feature their works on adequately elevated platforms unless, of course, they were well-established faculty members at regional colleges and universities. Some, though not all, of these illustrious local academicians (including one or two of their tenure groveling subordinates) were not altogether keen on the idea of this grassroots organization getting its feet off the ground, since it undoubtedly posed a tenable threat to the exclusive territorial fiefdoms over which these Masters of the Universe held unbounded sovereignty. The esteemed academicians were virtually the only composers at the time whose names appeared on local marquees (in a manner of speaking) and by default the only ones in the region whose compositions received performances by subsidized domestic ensembles specializing in contemporary classical music, notwithstanding that they were not necessarily any more gifted or accomplished than a good many of their freelance counterparts eking out their careers in the local ghetto. A sort of coup d'état was attempted by these academicians (a wholesale effort to sabotage what Bernstein and his contingent had been striving so hard to accomplish), which necessitated the Bernstein contingent holding clandestine meetings in undisclosed cavernous locations around town to ensure that the organization would be officially constituted with its intended charter intact. A power struggle of sorts ensued in the year or so prior to Cascadia Composers' inaugural concert. While the founding members of the group held their secret sessions, the esteemed university faculty composers continued to attend what they had mistakenly assumed were the bona fide monthly gatherings of the group, most probably thinking (with the smug complacency not atypical of those who delude themselves into imagining they are somehow mystically entitled by their privileged status) that they had effectively succeeded, through the agency of their grandiose Machiavellian schemes, in usurping upon the domain of Bernstein and his contingent and therethrough felicitously corrupting the organization's intended agenda to fit their own quasi-nefarious self- (if not pelf-) serving ends. What eventuated was a smartly calculated sleight-of-hand trick on the part of the Bernstein contingent to efficaciously counter the treacherous ambush by these pestiferous academicians (and one or two of their tenure-groveling subordinates)—a classic sting operation insofar as its having successfully swept the carpet out from under their feet, for, almost immediately upon ascertaining that their unscrupulous scheme had backfired upon them, these perfidious career-mongers dispersed themselves all aflutter, like a yech! of inquisitive cockroaches caught in the blinding glare of an attentional spotlight. What made this episode particularly unsettling to this author was to witness firsthand the extraordinary extent to which these totalitarian control freaks exerted themselves in an effort to usurp command of the original group for the purpose of satisfying their own insatiable lust for power, for while they attempted this takeover of what was rightfully and legitimately Professor Bernstein's operation, seeing as he had executed all the initial footwork in a strenuous campaign to bring his powerful vision for the organization to full fruition, these cloistered schoolmen were engaged in blatant Lord-of-the-Flies maneuvers with the object of assuming a kind of dictatorial dominance over Bernstein's enterprise. These territorial academicians almost literally shoved the group's founder aside from his position of leadership (or so they thought), notwithstanding that he was the group's principal founder and organizer. (Bernstein was a retired Professor of Composition from the University of Akron in Ohio who had, at the time, only recently moved with his wife to the Portland metro area and was most probably viewed for that reason, by certain of his opportunistic if not unprincipled local colleagues —howsoever uncollegially—as a menacingly dangerous "new kid on the block.") Of course, the names of the culpable parties—to wit: those involved in the plotted coup attempt—will not be printed here. One can only assume that the prime instigators of the aforetold ploy would beg to differ with the present account of what had transpired in the heady days leading up to the historically consequential founding of Cascadia Composers, seeing as they wouldn't wish to have their immaculate reputations besmirched in any way, shape, or form. Suffice it to say that one adverse outcome of this foiled attempt by the powers (and kowtowers) in office to quell the launch of this grassroots organization is that their monikers no longer appear on local marquees with quite the same level of incidence as they had in bygone days.... Simply put, for all intents and purposes, these conniving machinators had shot themselves in the foot, for their statuses as cardinal slumlords of the new music tenderloin had been downgraded a peg or three (an aftereffect of their attempts to suppress rather than embrace an organization that was meant to benefit their less privileged bedfellows in the community), which gives rise to not entirely unschadenfreudistic sentiments on the part of not only this author but many others who found themselves caught off guard by the predatorial incursion of these entitled prima donnas into the more rugged terrain of their institutionally unaffiliated colleagues). In any case, not wishing to digress any further from the principal topic at hand, it is incumbent upon this author to revisit the opuscule under discussion. (Ahem....) The review of Noland's WALTZ FANTASY in Willamette Week described the work as "a modern twist on a Strauss-style waltz" while the Northwest Reverb review read "... Like an André Rieu opium dream, Noland's waltz slowly emerged from a morass of sound, solidified into a lush, decadent, Viennese waltz before dissolving and reforming again and again. Like Bernstein, Noland made great use of the familiar, in this case the easily recognized waltz form, but made it personal, unique...." A grainy recording of that historic performance, as well as a studio recording of a tolerable mechanical rendition thereof, may be accessed on the composer's YouTube channel via the following link: https://www.youtube.com/c/GaryNoland/videos?view=0&sort=da&flow=grid

KORNGOLDAROONIE for string trio (violin, viola & cello) Op. 94 was composed as a tribute to composer Erich Wolfgang Korngold (1897-1957) and was commissioned by Marzena for the Free Marz String Trio with funding support from the Baby LeRoy Memorial Trust. The contemporary classical concert series Seventh Species, which Noland founded in San Francisco in 1990, featured the world premiere of KORNGOLDAROONIE on March 23rd, 2011 at Sherman-Clay Recital Hall in Portland's Pearl District, which was attended by Korngold's granddaughter Katy Korngold Hubbard, the cello part having been played by her husband John Hubbard. Also featured on that concert was the U.S. premiere of Korngold's piano arrangement for four hands of his Piano Trio Op. 1 by pianists Kaori Katayama Noland (Noland's wife) and Mio Aoike, a work that received its world premiere in Vienna almost exactly one hundred years prior thereto (in the selfsame month) by none other than E.W. Korngold himself and Bruno Walter. According to Korngold scholar Brendan Carroll, "…there was a gala performance of the Trio scheduled for March 1911 in Vienna. Friedrich Buxbaum (the great cellist) was ill and could not play and as the Brahmsaal [at Musikverein, Vienna] was fully sold out, there was suddenly a crisis. After much discussion, it was decided that there was just no time for another cellist to learn the very difficult part & then join Arnold Rose and Bruno Walter and be able to rehearse it adequately, in the time left … so young Korngold (not yet 14!) boldly decided to make a 4 hand version for Walter and himself to play instead, and thus saved the concert! This Korngold did, in about 48 hours—and it was such a success, that UE decided to publish that version too. However, I have no record of it being performed again!" A performance of KORNGOLDAROONIE by violinist Corinne Stillwell, violist Pamela Ryan, and cellist Dorien De León that took place at the Portland Community Music Center on June 18, 2011, may heard at the following link: https://soundcloud.com/gary-noland/korngoldaroonie-for-string-trio-op-94. Another performance of KORNGOLDAROONIE by violinist Lucia Conrad, violist Marissa Winship, and cellist Diane Chaplin that was recorded in Portland on November 23rd, 2014, may be heard on YouTube. IRRATIONALISMUS for cello & piano Op. 96 (2010) was commissioned by pianist Cristina Cavalli and cellist Antonino Saladino and received its world premiere by aforesaid duo in March, 2011 at the Teatro Nuovo Colosseo in Rome, Italy. Cellist Diane Chaplin and pianist Cary Lewis performed the U.S. premiere some six months later, on September 17th, 2011, on a Cascadia Composers concert in Portland, Oregon. Unfortunately, the composer was unable to attend either of those concerts. However, he was able to attend a later performance (made possible, in part, by generous funding from Portland composer Daniel Brugh), on March 22nd, 2019, at Lincoln Hall, Portland State University by cellist Avery Waite and pianist Jeff Payne on a Cascadia Composers concert celebrating the (then) tenth anniversary of the group's founding. That rendition of IRRATIONALISMUS may be heard at the following link: https://composergarynoland.godaddysites.com/music-videos-1-1.

BIRCHERMUESLI: "Cereal Music" for string quartet, Op. 6 (1986) was premiered by the Freeland Quartet (a pickup ensemble) at Paine Hall, Harvard University on Valentine's Day, 1986. The composer had spent many hours prior to that performance preparing a huge vat of Swiss-style Birchermuesli to feed his audience at the reception following the concert. Composer Ivan Tcherepnin (son of Alexander Tcherepnin) was present at the reception and shared with the composer that he was a personal friend of the Bircher family in Switzerland, descendants of Maximilian Oskar Bircher-Benner (1867-1939), the Swiss physician who popularized muesli. As a strapping young buck of thirteen, Noland had been initiated into the world of muesli at the Möwenpick in Zürich in September, 1970, and has, ever since, been an avid fan of the cereal-based gruel.

ROMANCE for viola & piano Op. 10 is one of Noland's most popular works. Paradoxically, at the time he composed it (1980-81), he was maliciously ridiculed by a number of individuals from both inside and outside the academic music establishment for composing a piece so unabashedly romantic in character, as doing so was considered immoral by the puritanical modernists of that period who were of the collective ideological mindset that functional harmony, when-and-wheresoever it reared its "ugly" head, was déclassé, hence nugatory (of course, that was on a different planet in another century). Noland heard through the grapevine that his ROMANCE had been performed in jest by some students (approximately forty years ago at the time of this writing) at a party (to which he hadn't been invited) hosted by a distinguished composition professor amidst the scornful mockery of both said professor and his impressionable young neophytes (both undergraduate and graduate students alike). The censure of this work, in fact, was so violently contemptuous, it cost Noland one or two friendships (no great loss, as it turns out, for the composer had zero tolerance for disloyalty). All the same, the ROMANCE has proven, in the forty years since its inception, to possess an exceptional staying power, which is no mean feat in the corrupt and chaotic world of contemporary art music. A number of musicians have expressed to Noland over the years their unshakable conviction that his ROMANCE is destined to become a staple in the viola literature. Until the publication of this collection, the score of this piece had been difficult to come by, in spite of frequent requests from violists, as it had been in very limited circulation over the years. It was first recorded for North Pacific Music by violist Rozanna Weinberger and pianist Evelyne Luest (wife of Pulitzer prize winning composer Aaron Kernis) at Ball State University, Muncie, Indiana in September, 1994. Another recording of the piece, made by violist Katherine Murdock and pianist Randall Hodgkinson at the home of Paul Matisse (grandson of Henri Matisse and stepson of Marcel Duchamp) in Groton, MA, just outside of Boston, in November, 1987, may be heard at the following link: https://soundcloud.com/gary-noland/sets/ romance-for-viola-piano-op-10. That performance is included on a compilation CD of Noland's compositions titled SELECTED MUSIC FROM VENGE ART, which can be ordered from North Pacific Music at: http://www.northpacificmusic.com/VengeArt.html. The ROMANCE was more recently performed (in the spring of 2021) by violist Vladimir Bistritsky and pianist Zlata Olyunina at the Church Hall of Sheremetev Palace at the St. Petersburg Museum of Music on a piano owned by Dmitry Shostakovich (!). Here is a link to that performance (the plaque seen atop the piano attests to Shostakovich's ownership of the instrument): https://www.facebook.com/vladimir.bistritsky/videos/3788377427946168.

At a mere two pages, and thus devoid of the necessity of any page turns, the score of POCKET TRIO for violin, cello & piano Op. 79 is sufficiently concise and self-contained to function as both score and parts for all three players.

INTERMEZZO for violin & piano Op. 18 received its world premiere on a Seventh Species concert at Mills College on October 26th, 1991 by violinist Reiko Nishioka with the composer at the piano. It was later performed by violinist Leslie Sawyer (then Concert Master of the Eugene Symphony) and the composer's wife Kaori Katayama Noland on a Seventh Species concert at Lane Community College in Eugene, Oregon on March 22, 1997 and then later on a Seventh Species concert at Flannagan Chapel, Lewis & Clark College in Portland, Oregon on October 24th, 1997. INTERMEZZO was later performed by violinist Ron Blessinger (Artistic Director of the Third Angle Ensemble, Executive Director of 45th Parallel, and violinist in the Oregon Symphony) and pianist Jennifer Garrett at Newport Center for the Performing Arts on a Composers Symposium Concert at the Ernest Bloch Music Festival in Newport, Oregon on June 30th, 2004 (when Bernard Rands was the resident composer of the festival).

DOG DUO Op. 66a (2002) is scored for viola and cello as well as for clarinet and bassoon Op. 66b. It received its first performance as a reading/recording by violist Nicola Boag and cellist Carolina Gomez of the ACM (Accessible Contemporary Music) Ensemble in Chicago, Illinois on January 6th, 2005. The clarinet/bassoon version of this piece (Op. 66b) was performed on November 18th, 2006 by clarinetist Ben Farrell and bassoonist Richard Essenberg at a Cherry Blossom Arts Salon at Tsunami Books, in Eugene, Oregon. An electronicized version of this piece was released on the CD titled ROYAL OILWORKS MUSIC in 2006, which is available from North Pacific Music at: http://www.northpacificmusic.com/noland.oilworks.html. It may be heard at the following link:

https://soundcloud.com/gary-noland/dog-duo-op-66. The viola/cello version received its West Coast premiere on a Seventh Species concert titled "A June Night Swoon of Torrid Tunes" at the Community Music Center in Portland by violist Pamela Ryan and cellist Dorien De León on June 18th, 2011. That performance can be heard on the composer's YouTube channel. It was later recorded in Italy in an arrangement by bass-clarinetist Sauro Berti and contrabassoonist Fabio Morbidelli for bass clarinet and contrabassoon. That recording is scheduled for release in the near future on a double CD of Noland's compositions titled MUSIC OF RAGE, SORROW, LOVE, LAUGHTER & BUREAUCRACY.

An early unpublished version of FANTASY IN E MINOR for cello & piano Op. 24 was premiered by cellist Scott Kluksdahl and pianist Brian Marble in May, 1984 at Paine Hall, Harvard University. Noland revised the piece eight years later (in 1992). The newly revised version was recorded and performed by cellist Hamilton Cheifetz and pianist Victor Steinhardt at Beall Hall, University of Oregon on September 11th, 1998, and released in the summer of 2002 by North Pacific Music on the CD SELECTED MUSIC FROM VENGE ART. That performance may be heard at either of the following links: https://soundcloud.com/gary-noland/sets/fantasy-in-e-minor-for-cello or https://www.youtube.com/results?search_query=fantasy+in+e+minor+noland. The FANTASY IN E MINOR was later performed on July 26th, 2002 by cellist Phil Hansen and pianist Jennifer Garrett at the Newport Center for the Performing Arts on a Composers Symposium Concert at the Ernest Bloch Music Festival in Newport, Oregon (when David Del Tredici was the resident composer of the festival). Over the years Noland has received numerous requests for the score, which he was usually unable to provide due to the sheer expense and inconvenience of doing so. Now, with the publication of this collection, that issue will finally, it is hoped, be resolved.

FUGUE IN G MAJOR for string quartet Op. 13 was originally composed in 1978 as an open score for unspecified instrumentation, then later scored for string orchestra. This was done at a time when composing fugues was unfashionable, even frowned upon by the cacademic lamestream. In those days one risked being ostracized by one's colleagues for writing a fugue if one treated the process as anything more ambitious in scope than that of the mere scratching out of a pedagogically mediocre lab exercise, notwithstanding that those who view the process as such tend to know very little about the enormous set of skills it takes to write a fugue worth its salt. The string orchestra version of FUGUE IN G MAJOR received its premiere performance at Assembly Hall, Boston Conservatory under the baton of Francis Léger in 1982. It was later performed as a reading by the Harvard-Radcliffe Orchestra String Section at Sanders Theatre, Harvard University under James Yannatos. Noland thereupon revised the piece and published it in a string quartet version in 1989. That version received its premiere on a Seventh Species concert at Mills College on February 21st, 1991 by the Magellan String Quartet (Ron Erickson, 1st violin; ◎India Cooke, 2nd violin; Meg Titchener, viola; and Matt Brubeck [son of the legendary jazz pianist David Brubeck], cello). It was later performed on a Seventh Species concert at the Newman Center in Eugene, Oregon on June 22nd, 2000 by violinists Anthony Dyer and Jennifer Cowell, violist Andrew Justice, and cellist Mintcho Badev.

Table of Contents

Gary Noland
Waltz Fantasy
for Violin & Piano
Op. 87

Freeland Publications

FP119

Waltz Fantasy

for violin & piano

by Gary Noland, Op. 87

17
A
mf
mf
Ped.
20
f
mp
f
mp
23
f
f

25
mf
f
28
3:2
5:4
B
ff
sfz
31
mp
p

34
sf
p
mf
37
8va
tr
ff
dim.
41
3:2
mp
mf

Viennese waltz style
C
46
51
mp
cresc.
p
cresc.
57
D
f
mf

61
65
cresc.
cresc.
con bravura
piu lento
70
E
ff
f
8va
piu lento
fff
f

75
8va
78
rit. a tempo
(8va)
rit. a tempo
81
rit. a tempo
rit. a tempo
molto rit.
cresc.
(8va)
rit. a tempo
rit. a tempo
molto rit.
cresc.

84
a tempo
a tempo
ff
(8va)
fff
86
F
Tempo 1
ff
8va
Ped.
Ped.
88
f
f
mf
mf
mp
cresc.
Ped.

93
f
mp
mf
f
f
p
cresc.
f
L.H.
mp
S.P.
100
mp
mf
f
cresc.
R.H.
f
dim.
p
106
p
f
mp
ff
mf
f
mf

112
poco dim.
f
ff
f
116
mf
cresc.
f
120
G
ff
mf
p
dim.
mf

124
cresc.
f
p
cresc.
mf
130
f
mf
f
cresc.
ff
f cresc.
H mit Schmerz
136
mf
p
mf
ff
mf
p
mf

141
Pizz.
p
mp
f
mf
147
arco
mp
f
p
mf
153
ff
mp
mf
p

158
I
p
mf
mp
163
f
ff
f
167
mf
dim.
p
mf
mp
mf
dim.
p
mp

171
J
mf
mp
mf
175
mp
f
mf
mp
179
cresc.
f
Ped.

182
ff
dim.
sfz
ff
dim.
185
K
mf
mf
Ped.
188
mp
p
mf
mp
p
cresc.
3
8

192
f
mp
mf
199
3:2
205
p
Ped.

211
L
f
mp
f
mp
pochiss. rit.
220
p
cresc.
f
p
cresc.
f
a tempo
227
mf
dim.
p
mf
dim.
p

233
M
mf
f
dim.
mf
f
dim.
239
mp
cresc.
mf
mp
244
cresc. poco a poco
cresc. poco a poco

8va
249
ff
ff
(8va)
N
254
3/4
f
sfz
f
8va
f
8va
258
mf
f

261
mf
poco cresc.
mf
poco cresc.
265
ff
dim.
f
268
mf
poco cresc.
O
ff
dim.

273
278
283
3
f
mf
mp
p

288
ff
mf
f
f
mf
f
293
mp
Pizz.
f
arco
ff
mp
mf
mp
302
Pizz.
P
arco
f
p
Ped.

313
Pizz.
mf
arco
f
Ped.
Ped.
Ped.
318
Pizz.
mf
arco
mp
mf
Ped.
Ped.
324
Q
mp
p
Ped.
Ped.
Ped.

329
f
mp
f
3
3
f
mp
f
3
3
3
3
333
mf
336
R
mf
p
mf

341
p
mf
346
mp
mf
351
p
f
mp
f

355
359
364
S

367
f
mp
mf
p
373
sf
p
8va
tr
377
ff
dim.
f
3:2

382
T
3:2
mp
p
386
mf
mp
389
f
mf
p
mf

394
U
mp cresc.
mp cresc.
402
f
p
mp
409
mf
f
cresc.
ff
cresc.

416
V
mf
f
mf
f
ff
mf
f
Ped.
421
ff
mf
427
W
8va
p
f
mp

(8va)
432
p
mf
436
dim.
p
441
mf
f
mp
8va
dolce

447
X
mf
p
mf
mp
mf
poco dim.
p
Ped.
453
f
ff
mp
mf
457
mf
8va
ff

Y
462
molto espressivo
(8va)
467
472

476
p
mf
poco dim.
480
Z
f
mp
mf
485
mp
cresc.
mp
cresc.

493
f
p
mf
Ped.
501
mp
cresc.
8va
506
(8va)
ff
AA
p
mp

510
cresc.
mp
515
f
p
mf
mf
f
p
mp
520
f
cresc.
f

525
p
mf
ff
p
mf
530
cresc.
f
f
BB
534
ff
mp
fff
dim.
p
ff
dim.

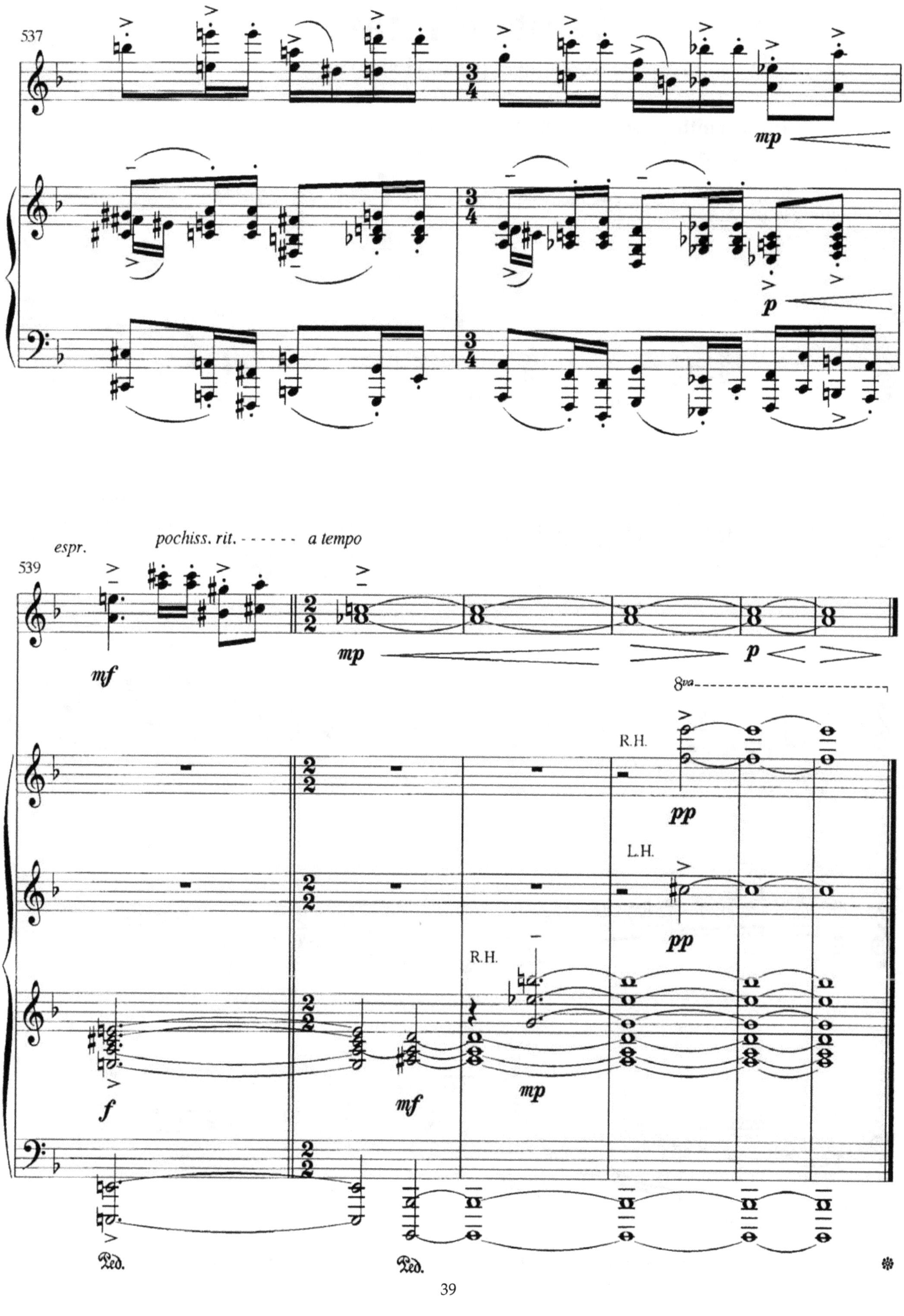

espr.
pochiss. rit. - - - - - - a tempo
539
mf
mp
p
8va
R.H.
pp
L.H.
pp
R.H.
f
mf
mp
Ped.
Ped.

Waltz Fantasy

for violin & piano: violin part

by Gary Noland, Op. 87

32
mp
mf

35
8va
tr
sf
p
ff

(8va)
39
dim.
3:2
mp

Viennese waltz style
C
43
p
mf

51
mp
cresc.
f

D
mf
cresc.
ff
con bravura
E
f
cresc.
ff
F
f
mf
f
f
mp
mf
f
mp
mf
f

105
p
f
mp
111
ff
poco dim.
116
mf
cresc.
ff
mf
G
p
cresc.
125
f
p
cresc.
f
mf
f
cresc.
133
ff
H
mit Schmerz
mf
p
mf
141
p
Pizz.
mp
f
mp
f
arco
mp
f
p
mf
149
p
ff
mp
154
ff
mf
p
p

I
5
f
ff
mf
dim.
p
mf
mp
J
mf
mp
f
mf
cresc.
ff
dim.
K
mf
mp
p
mf
3
8
f
mp
mf
3:2
f

204
p
211
L
f
mp
pochiss. rit.
a tempo
p
223
cresc.
f
mf
dim.
231
M
p
mf
f
dim.
mp
cresc.
240
mf
cresc. poco a poco
8va
248
N
ff
f
256
sfz
mf
f
mf
poco cresc.
263
ff
dim.

O
poco cresc.
Pizz.
arco
P
Q

331
mf
335
R
343
p
mf
mp
mf
351
p
f
mp
f
mf
356
ff
360
f
mp
3:2
5:4
365
S
ff
f
f
mp

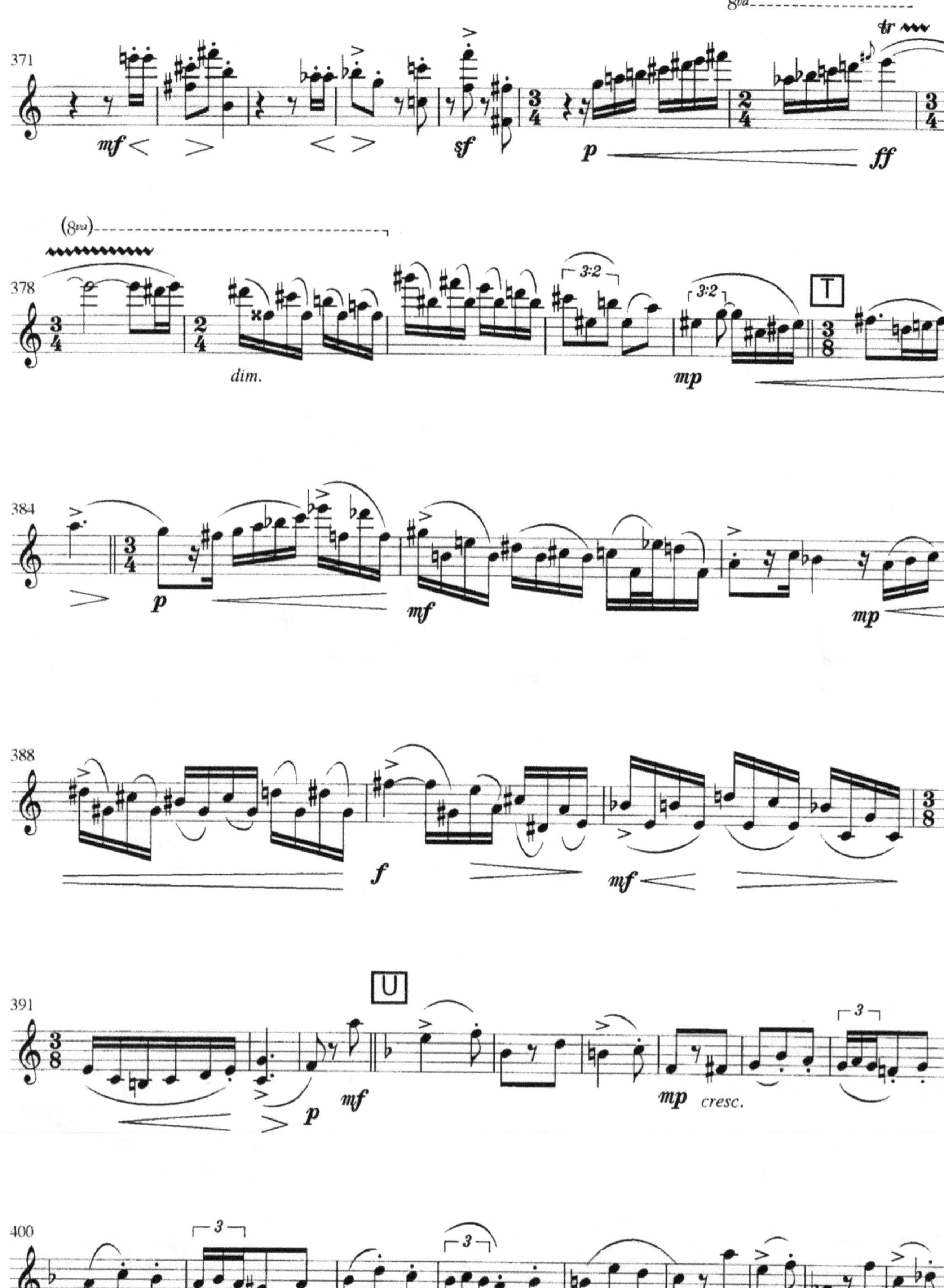
8va
371
mf
sf
p
ff
tr
(8va)
378
3:2
T
dim.
mp
384
p
mf
mp
388
f
mf
391
U
p
mf
mp
cresc.
3
400
f
p
mp

409
cresc.
417
V
422
8va
429
W
(8va)
433
dim.
(8va)
438
443
450
X

456
Y
ff
mf
f
463
molto espressivo
p
f
468
p
f
471
mp
f
p
475
f
p
479
f
Z
483
mp
cresc.
492
f
p
mf
mf

8va
501
mp
cresc.
ff
(8va)
507
AA
p
mp
512
cresc.
f
518
p
mf
524
f
p
mf
529
cresc.
f
BB
534
ff
mp
fff
dim.
espr.
pochiss. rit.
a tempo
538
mp
mf
mp
p

Gary Noland

KORNGOLDAROONIE

for String Trio

a Tribute to Erich Wolfgang Korngold

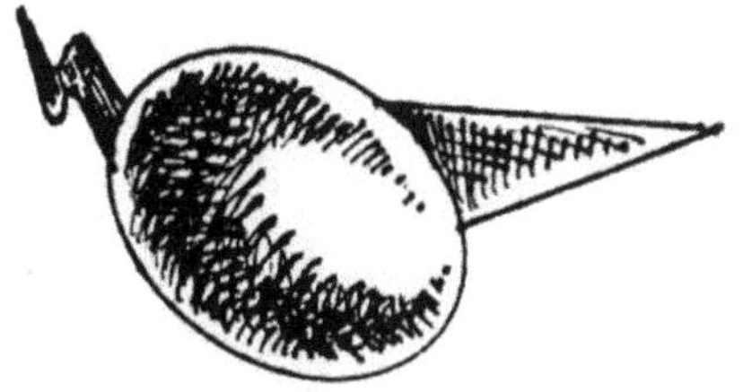

Op. 94

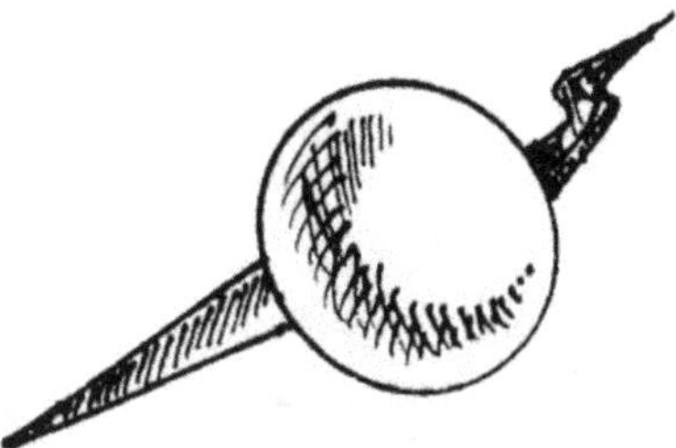

Commissioned by Marzena for the Free Marz String Trio
with funding support from the Baby LeRoy Memorial Trust

Freeland Publications

FP126

Korngoldaroonie

for string trio

a tribute to Erich Wolfgang Korngold

by Gary Noland, Op. 94

Duration: 3 minutes

Andantino sofisticato; avec recherche—mit *oomph!*

C
Vln.
Vla.
Vc.
espr.
D
schmalzy
Pizz.
arco
dim.

32
Vln.
Vla.
Vc.
p
ff
dim.
f
36
Pizz.
E
arco
mp
mf
p
41
dim.
46
F
cresc.

51
G
Vln.
Vla.
Vc.
ff
p
f
mp
mf
55
62
dim.
67

70
H
Vln.
Vla.
Vc.
Pizz.
Pizz.
76
I
arco
arco
espr.
80
J
espr.
Pizz.
arco
84

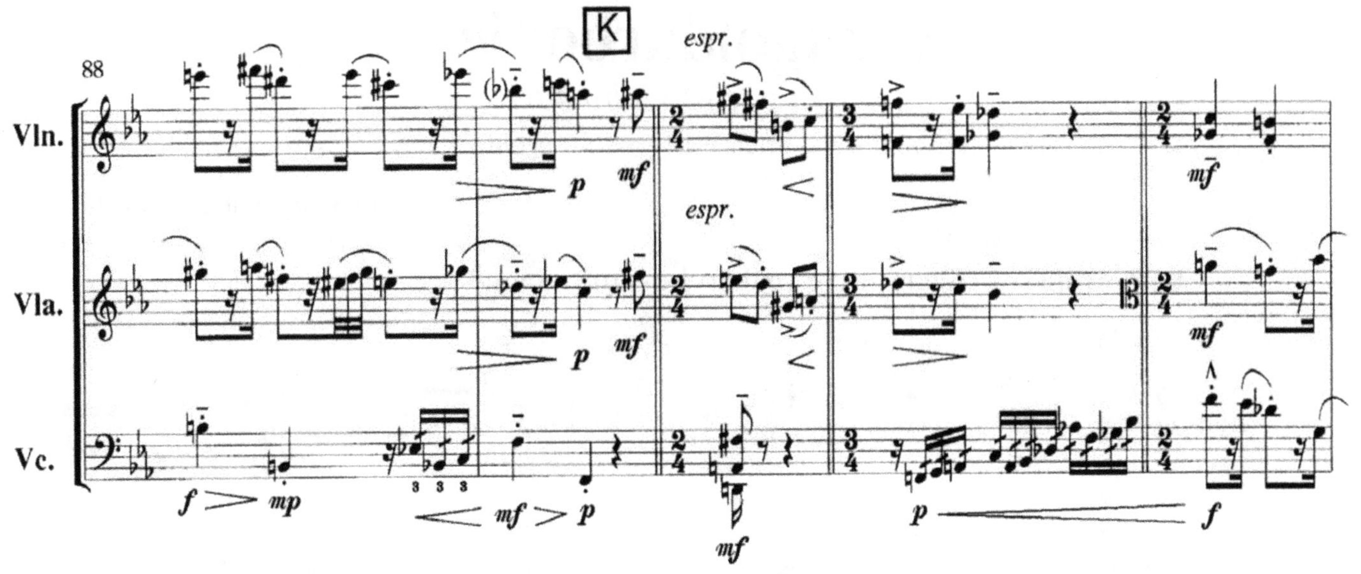
88
K
espr.
Vln.
Vla.
Vc.
espr.

93
L
Vln.
Vla.
Vc.
cresc.
cresc.
cresc.

97
Vln.
Vla.
Vc.

Korngoldaroonie

for string trio: violin part

a tribute to Erich Wolfgang Korngold

by Gary Noland, Op. 94

Duration: 3 minutes

Andantino sofisticato; avec recherche—mit *oomph!*

45
F
G
Vln.
f
mp
p cresc.
ff
53
mp
mf
p
mf
62
ff
dim.
mp
f
mf
67
p
f
71
H
mf
77
I
p
mf
f
80
J
mp
mf espr.
86
K
90
espr.
L
p cresc.
96
ff
mf
f
mp

Korngoldaroonie

for string trio: viola part

a tribute to Erich Wolfgang Korngold

by Gary Noland, Op. 94

Duration: 3 minutes

Andantino sofisticato; avec recherche—mit oomph!

46
Vla.
F
G
mp
p cresc.
ff
53
Vla.
mp
mf
p
mf
60
Vla.
p
ff
dim.
mp
mf
67
Vla.
p
f
p
71
Vla.
H
Pizz.
I
arco
f
mf
p
79
Vla.
J
mf
f
mp
f
mp
mf
espr.
83
Vla.
mf
p
f
88
Vla.
K
espr.
p
mf
92
Vla.
L
mf
p cresc.
97
Vla.
ff
mf
f
mp
mf
p

Korngoldaroonie

for string trio: cello part

a tribute to Erich Wolfgang Korngold

by Gary Noland, Op. 94

Duration: 3 minutes

Vc.
F
G
H
Pizz.
I
arco
J
Pizz.
arco
K
L
cresc.

Gary Noland

Irrationalismus

for cello & piano

Op. 96

Freeland Publications

FP128

Irrationalismus

for cello & piano

* All trills begin on the upper auxiliary.

dolce
40
mp
mf
mf
f
espr.
mf
mp
45
pp
mp
mf
mf
mf
mp
49
pochiss. dim.
mp
3:2
p poco cresc.

53
tr
mf
p
cresc. poco a poco
f
mp
mf
57
f
dim. poco a poco
Cantando
60
f
pochiss. dim.
mp
cresc. poco a poco
f

64
3:2
3:2
mf
p
poco cresc.
mf
f
mf
3:2
3:2
70
mf
f
ff
mp
cresc.
poco f
75
f
mp
mf
3
4

78
espr.
f
mf
sfz
82
con forza
pizz.
ff
mf
86
arco
pizz.
arco

90
port.
pizz.
mf
f
espr.
ff
94
mf
f
ff
98
arco
pizz.
f
mf
mp

103
arco
f
mf
107
mp
mf
p
114
saltando
3:2
6:4
saltando
3:2
6:4
mp
mf
p
poco decresc.

molto espressivo
122
espr.
130
spicc.
saltando
spicc.
saltando
spicc.
136
espr.
saltando

142
149
gliss.
153
pochiss. rit. - - - a tempo
pochiss. rit. - - - a tempo
poco f

157
mp
mf
4:3
mf
161
f
3:2
mf
f
165
sul pont.
mf
mp
cresc. poco a poco

(sul. pont.)
170
espr.
cresc. poco a poco
f
cresc. poco a poco
S.P.
175 (sul. pont.)
8va
178 (sul. pont.)
ff
(8va)
fff
8va
S.P.
S.P.

181
(sul. pont.)
8va
S.P.
(sul. pont.)
modo ordinario
184
ff
f
mf
3:2
Ped.

Irrationalismus

cello part

Cantando
pochiss. dim.
poco cresc.
cresc.
con forza
pizz.
arco
port.

118
saltando
saltando
molto espressivo
127
spicc.
saltando
spicc.
saltando
spicc.
135
espr.
saltando
141
149
gliss.
pochiss. rit. - - - - - - - a tempo
155
159

164
3:2
3:2
3:2
3:2
f
sul pont.
mf
(sul. pont.)
170
espr.
cresc. poco a poco
(sul. pont.)
175
ff
(sul. pont.)
modo ordinario
180
ff
ff

"BIRCHERMUESLI"
cereal music for string quartet
by Gary Noland
OPUS 6
Freeland Publications
Cambridge MA
Berkeley CA

"Birchermuesli" Opus 6

"cereal music" for string quartet.

by Gary Noland

10
arco
f
mf
20
Pizz.
arco
tr

3
Pizz.
arco
tr
30
3
3
3
3
tr

40
tr

rit. Sprightly waltz tempo.
50
mf
mf
mf
mf
f
60
f
f

70
mf
mf
mf
mf
mp
mf
f
80
3
3
3
3
3
3

3
3
3
3
3
mf
mf
f
90
mf
mf
3

rit.
mp
a tempo
100
mf
f

110
tr
mf
f
mp
120

130
molto rit.
Tempo I
p
mp
mf
sfz

140
Pizz.
arco
150
Pizz.
arco

160
tr
tr
Pizz.
arco
3

170
tr
tr

180
mp
mp
3
3
3
mf
mf
mf
mf
3

190
f
ff
dim.
mf
mp

rit. a tempo
mf
mp
mf
mf
mp
mf
mp
p
mf
mp
p
200
tr
mf
mp
mp
mf
f
f
f
f
ff
ff
ff
rit.

"Birchermuesli" for string quartet

Violin I

by Gary Noland, op. 6

rit.
50
Sprightly waltz tempo.
mf
60
f
mf
70
80
mp
mf
3
3
3
90
mf
3
rit.
a tempo
mp
mf
100
f

110
tr
mf
f
mf
3
mp
120
130
p
mp
molto rit.
Tempo I
mf
140
150
160
tr
3

170
180
mf
f
ff
dim.
f
dim.
190
mf
f
mf
f
mf
mp
mf
mp
rit.
a tempo
200
tr
f
rit.
ff

"Birchermuesli" for string quartet

violin II

by Gary Noland, op. 6

40
rit.
50
Sprightly waltz
tempo
60
70
80
90
rit.
a tempo
100

* tremolo optional

170
180
mp
mf
f
ff
190
rit.
200
a tempo
rit.

"Birchermuesli" for string quartet.

viola

by Gary Noland, op. 6

rit.
50
Sprightly waltz tempo
mf
60
f
mf
70
80
3
90
mf
rit.
mp
a tempo
100
mf

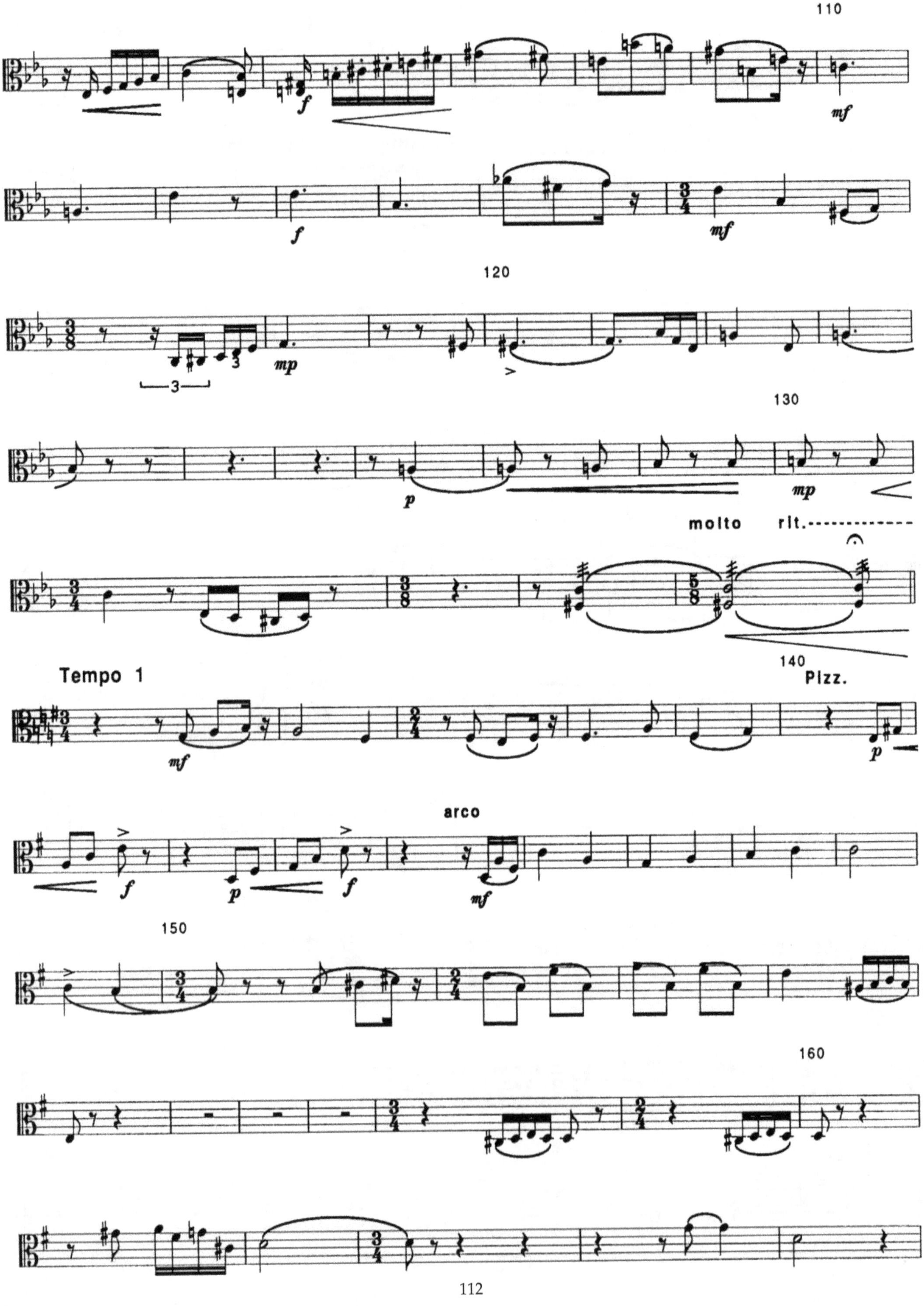
110
f
mf
f
mf
120
3
mp
130
p
mp
molto rit.
Tempo 1
mf
140
Pizz.
p
arco
f
p
f
mf
150
160

170
180
190
rit.
a tempo
200

"Birchermuesli" for string quartet

cello

by Gary Noland, op. 6

rit.
50
Sprightly waltz tempo.
mf
60
70
mf
80
mf
90
rit.
mp

a tempo
100
110
120
130
molto rit.
Tempo 1
140
150
Pizz.
arco
tr
Pizz.

160
arco
3
3
3
3
170
3
180
3
f
ff dim.
f dim.
mf
190
mf
f
f
mf
mf
mp
rit.
a tempo
p
200
mp
mf
f
rit.

Gary Noland

ROMANCE

for viola and piano

Opus 10

Freeland Publications

Romance

for viola and piano

by Gary Noland, Op. 10

dedicated to Rozanna Weinberger

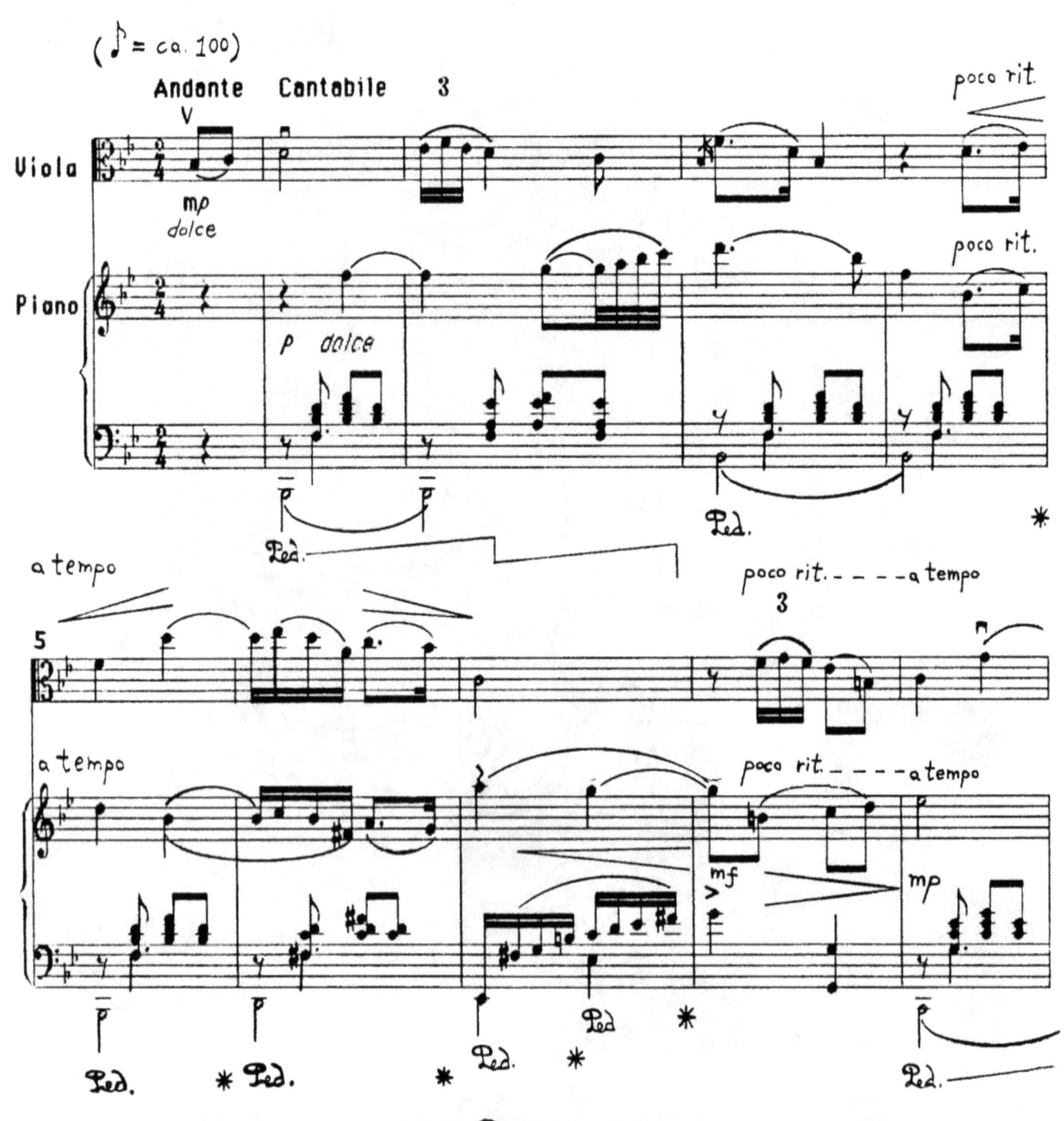

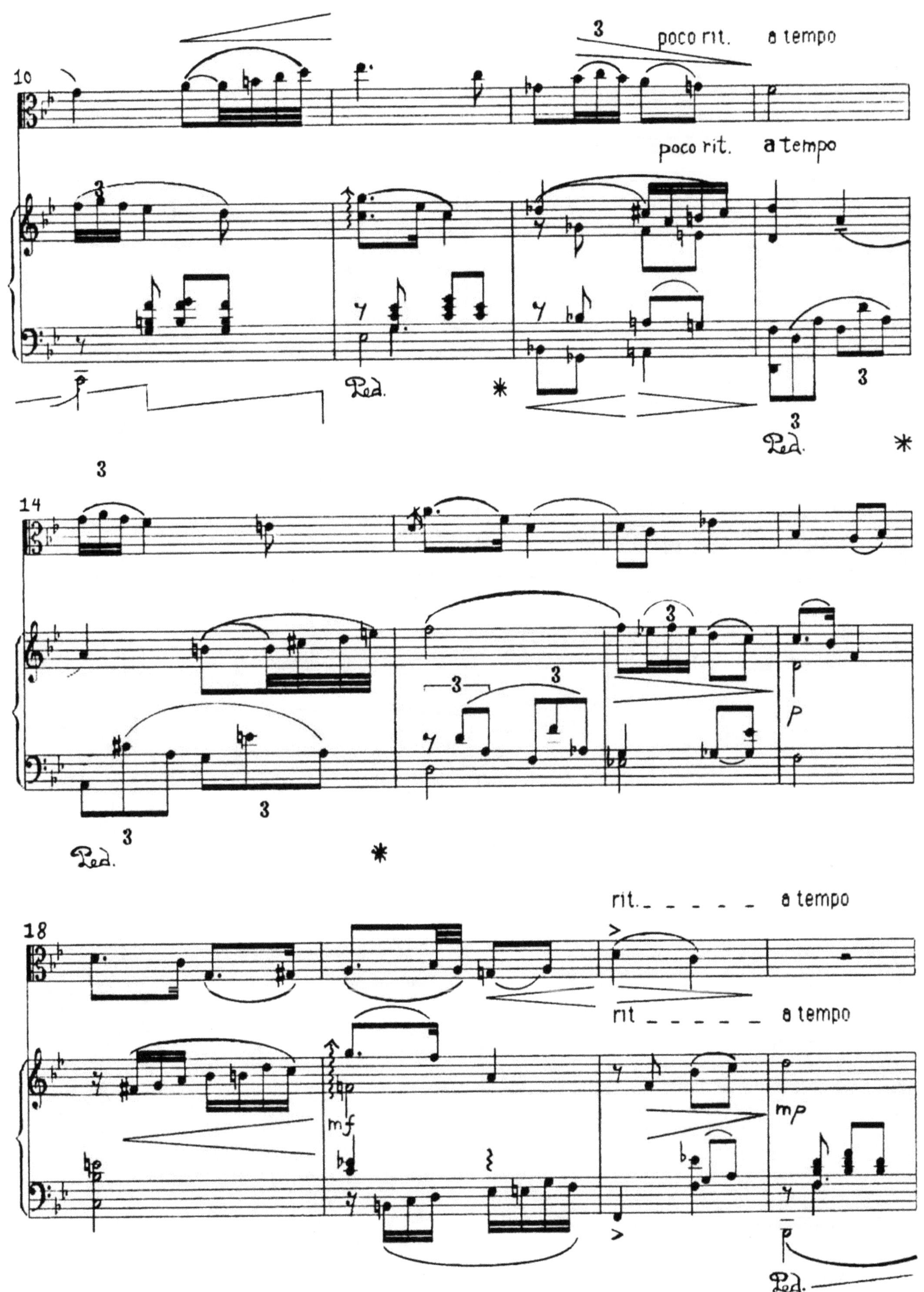

poco rit.
a tempo
poco rit.
a tempo
Ped.
Ped.
Ped.
rit.
a tempo
rit
a tempo
mf
mp
Ped.

22
6
6
mf
V
3
Ped.
Ped.
26
poco rit. _ _ _ a tempo
mf
poco rit. _ _ _ a tempo
3
mf
mp
3
3
Ped.
Ped.
Ped.
Ped.
30
3
3
f
3
3
3
3
Ped.
Ped.

poco rit. a tempo
33
poco rit.
a tempo
mp
37
f
f
39
mp
mf
mp

42
mp
rit.
rit.
mf
mp
p
Ped.
meno mosso (♪= ca. 88)
espressivo
46
mf
meno mosso
mp
5
3
3
Ped.
Ped.
Ped.
49
cresc.
cresc.
3
3
3
3
Ped.
Ped.

52
f
mp
3
f
dim.
mp
mf
Ped.
55
3
4
2
4
dim.
mp
57
mf
p
mp

59
61
mf
Ped.
63
rit.
rit.
dim.
mp
Ped.
Ped.

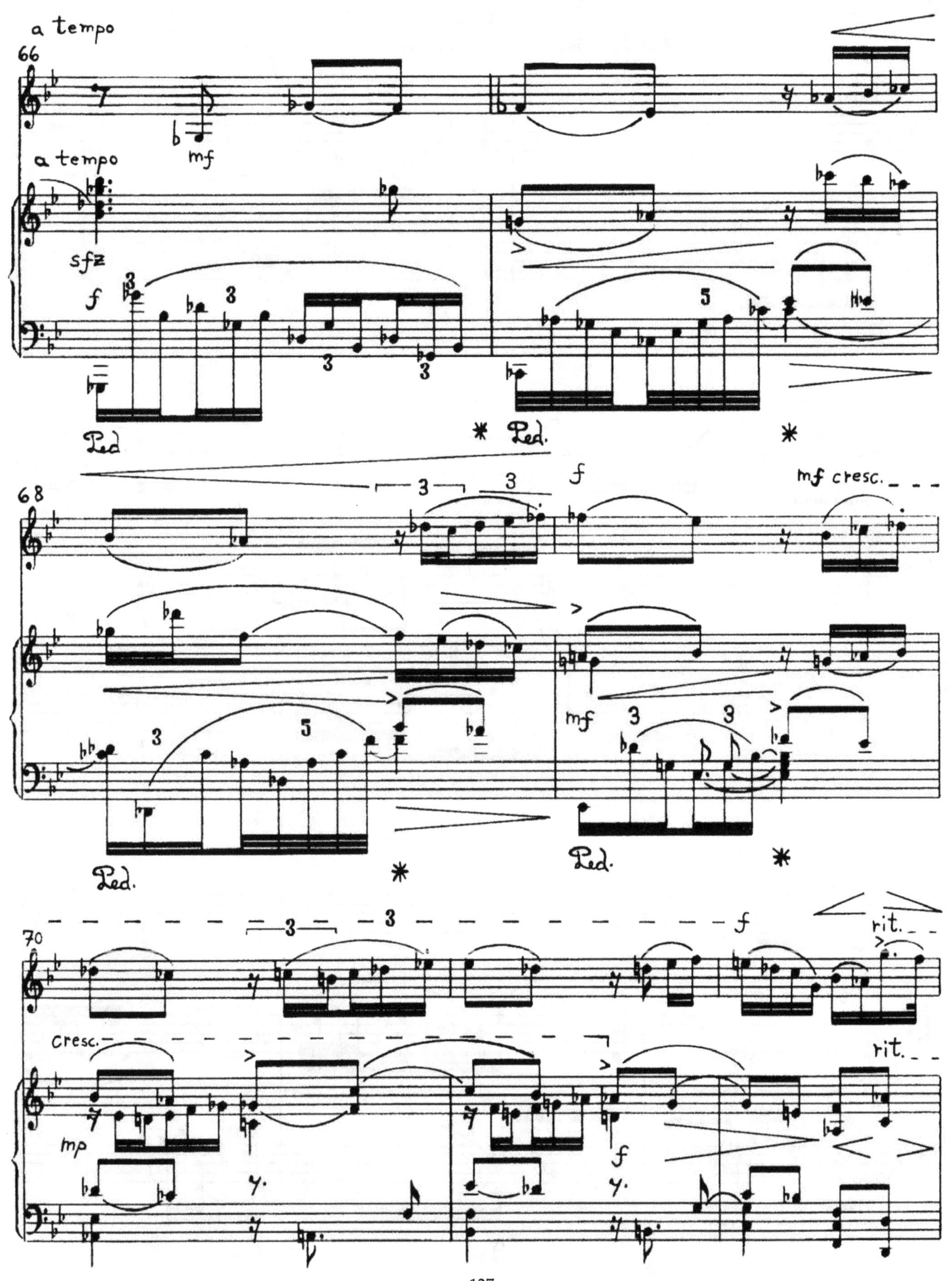
a tempo
66
mf
a tempo
sfz
f
Ped.
68
f
mf cresc.
mf
70
cresc.
mp
f
rit.

a tempo
poco rit.
mf
a tempo
mf
mp
Ped.
a tempo
mp
a tempo
p
mp
Ped.
p
mp
Ped.

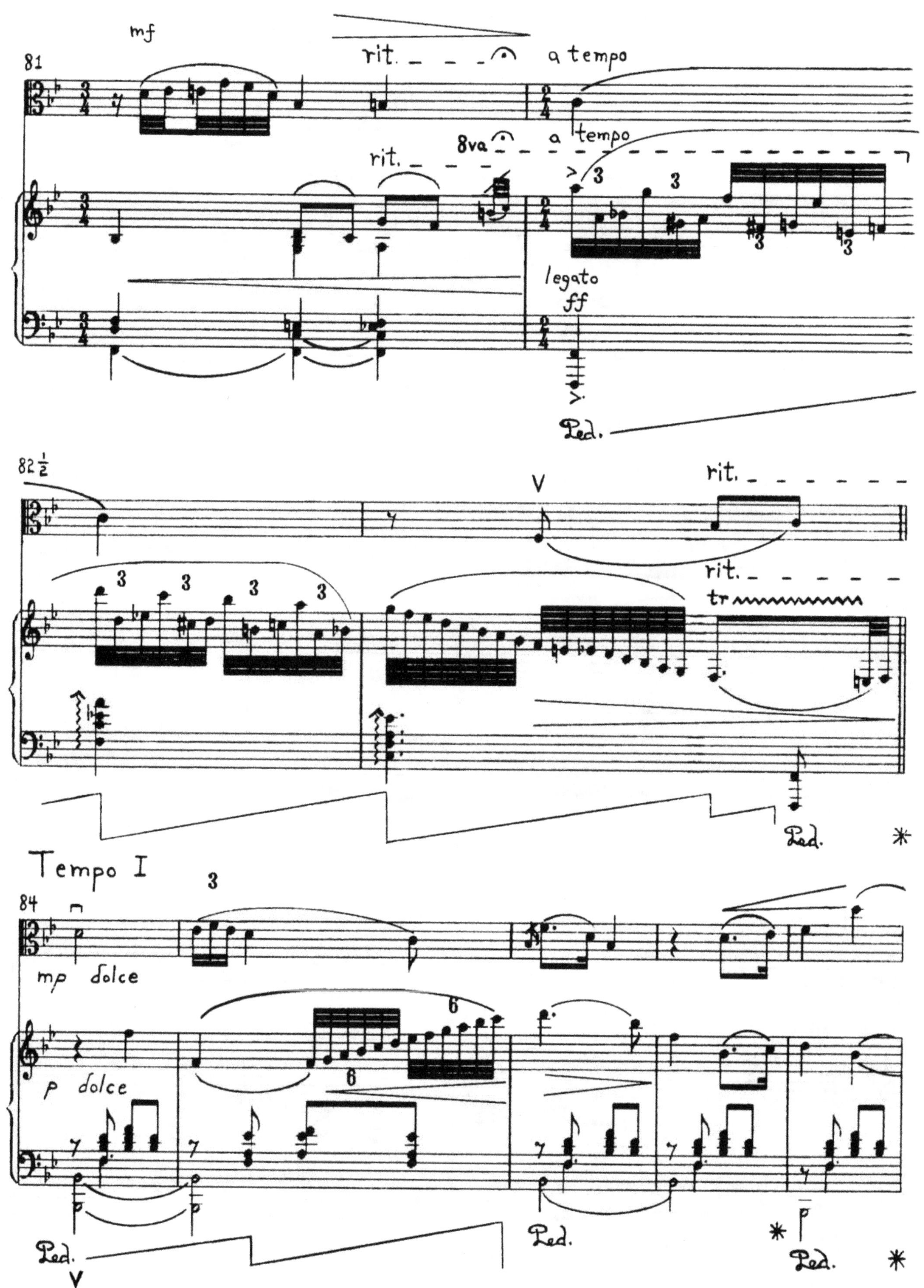
mf
rit.
a tempo
81
8va
rit.
a tempo
legato
ff
Ped.
82 1/2
rit.
rit.
tr
Ped.
Tempo I
84
mp dolce
p dolce
Ped.
Ped.
Ped.

poco rit. - - a tempo
poco rit. - - a tempo
mf
mp
Ped.
mf
poco rit.
poco rit.
a tempo
a tempo
p
p

ac - cel - er
101
mp
ac - cel - er
p
mp
an - do - poco - a
104
mp
an - do - poco - a
f
mp cresc.
poco
108
mf
poco
mf

112
f
mp
mp
mf
115
mf
f
mp
V
118
3
3
3
mf

(♪ = ca. 160 – 168)
121
ff
ff
122½
5
mf
mp cresc.
125
f

rit.
f
126½
rit.
mp
mf
(♪ = ca. 100)
meno mosso
129
a tempo poco a poco (from ♪ = 80 – ♪ = 100)
meno mosso
fff
mf
legato
3
Ped.
130½
7

(♪=ca. 76–80)
Adagio
131½
f
Adagio
ff
Ped.
(♪=ca. 88)
Andantino
cresc.
133
mf
Andantino
cresc.
mf
f
Ped.
136
ff
mf
f
dim.
mf
Ped.

139
dim.
dim.
mp
p
Ped.
Ped.
141
mp
dim.
p
mp
dim.
tr
Ped.
144
tr
tr
p
p cresc.
Ped.
* trills should begin on the upper auxiliary note.

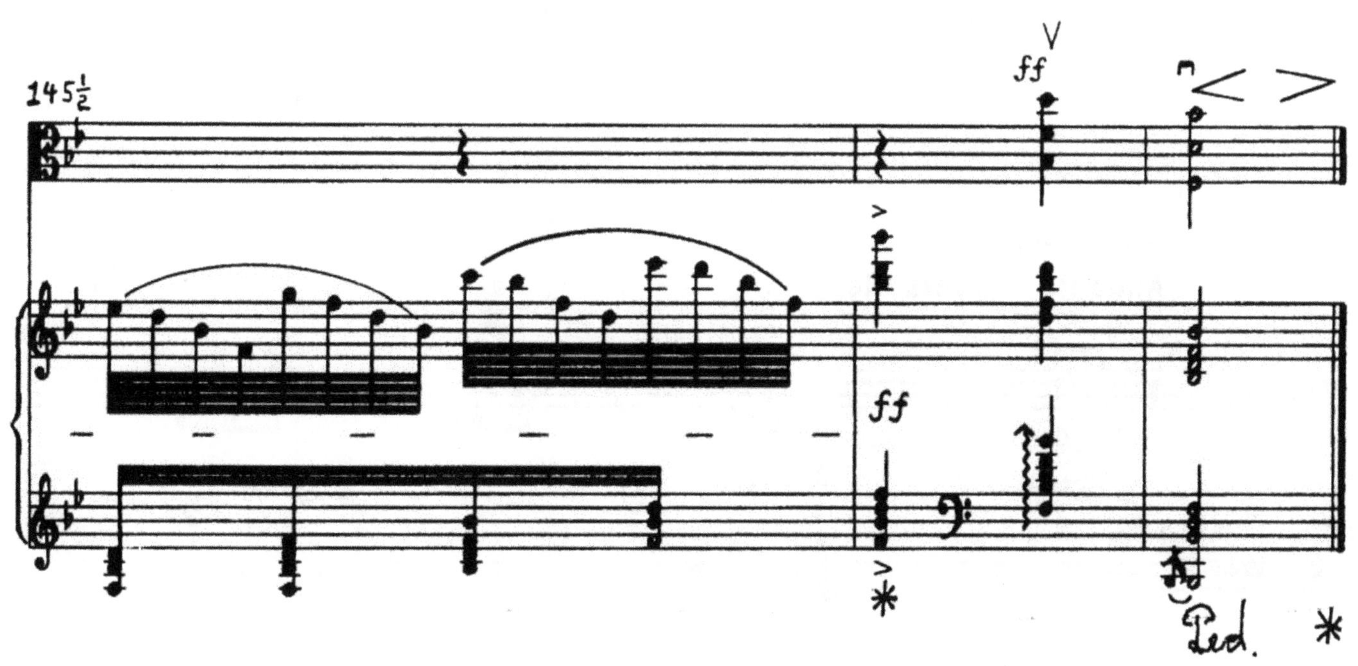
145½
ff
ff
Ped.

Romance

for viola and piano, viola part

by Gary Noland, op. 10

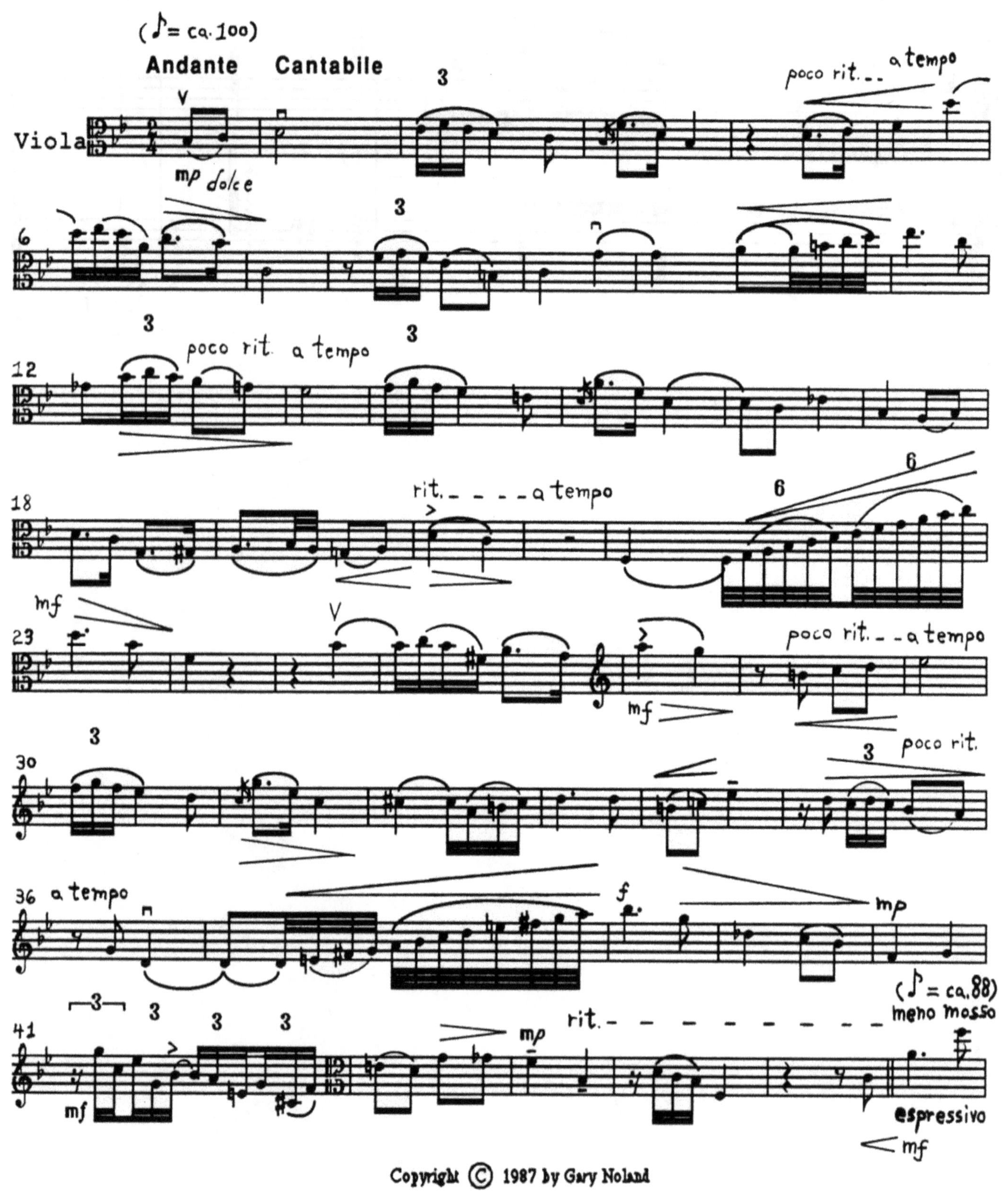

cresc.
f
mp
mf
mf cresc.
rit.
a tempo
poco rit. a tempo
p
rit. a tempo
rit.
Tempo I
mp dolce
poco rit. a tempo
poco rit. a tempo

* trills should begin on the upper auxiliary note.

Gary Noland

POCKET TRIO

for violin, cello & piano

Op. 79

Freeland Publications

FP110

Pocket Trio

for violin, cello & piano

by Gary Noland, Op. 79

C
D
Vln.
Vc.
Pno.
modo ord.
pochiss. rit. - - - - -
poco

Gary Noland
Op. 18
Intermezzo
for violin and piano
G. Noland 7/23/90
Freeland Publications

Intermezzo

for violin and piano

by Gary Noland
op. 18

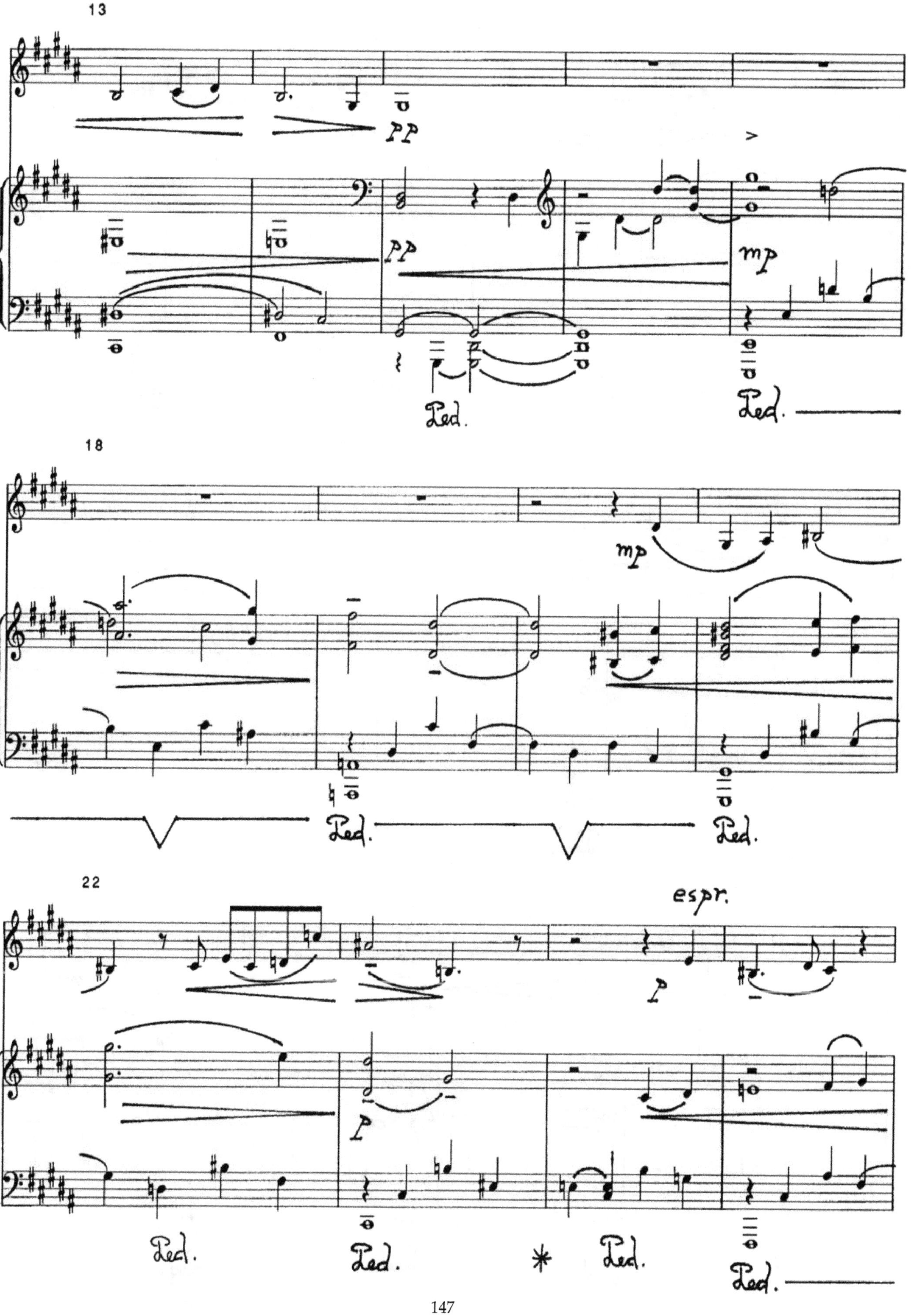

13
pp
pp
mp
Ped.
Ped.
18
mp
Ped.
Ped.
22
espr.
p
p
Ped.
Ped.
*
Ped.
Ped.

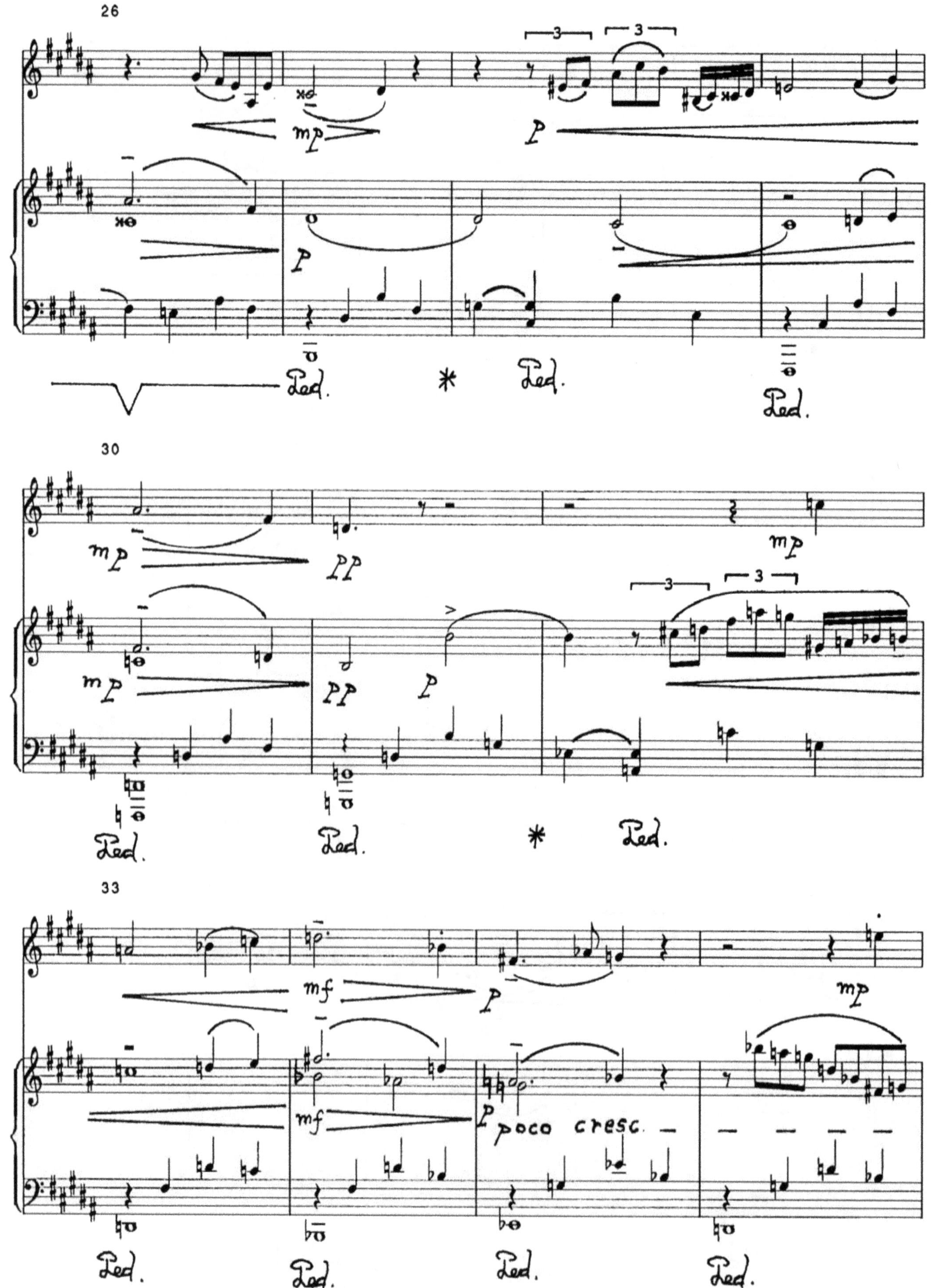
26
mp
p
Ped.
30
mp
pp
p
33
mf
poco cresc.

37
mf
f
(cresc.)
f
Ped.
Ped.
40
mp
mf
mf
44
mp
mf
mp
mf

48
rit.
a tempo
dolce
mp
mf
rit.
a tempo
dolce
mp
Ped.
53
7
Ped.
57
5
6
mp
p
Ped.
Ped.

60
mp
5
Ped.
63
6
mf
66
f

69
3
3
3
6
mf
7
mf
Ped.
71
5
Ped.
Ped.
Ped.
74
6
f
f
Ped.
Ped.
Ped.

77
p cresc.
f
mp
ff
Ped.
Ped.
Ped.
Ped.
82
poco dim.
mf
poco dim
f
88
mp
(poco dim.)
poco dim.

93
mp
99
(poco dim.)
cresc.
poco a poco
105
pp
mf
mp

112
118
Pizz.
arco
poco meno mosso
125
poco rit. _ Ländlich
(rustic)
poco meno mosso
poco rit. _ Ländlich
(rustic)

129
pp
Ped.
133
mp
p
mp
Ped.
Ped.
Ped.
3
136
mf
Ped.

139
143
146
mf
p
mp
Ped.

149
152
155
Ped.
mp

158
dolce
mf
p
Ped.
161
mp
Ped.
Ped.
163
mf
f
mf
f
Ped.
Ped.
Ped.

166
mf
mf
169
f
mp
Ped.
Ped.
171
5
mf
f
mf
mf
Ped.

174
arco
177
f
mf
181
ff
mf dim.

186
mf
p
mf
p
f
sfz
mp
Ped.
S.P.
189
3
Ped.
Ped.
(S.P.)
191
p cresc.
p cresc.
Ped.
(S.P.)

193
(cresc.)
(cresc.)
195
mf
mf
197
ff
ff
f

199
mp
mf sfz p cresc.
poco a poco
Ped.
Ped.
sfz
S.P.
202
cresc.
204
f
ff
f

208
f
mf
212
mf
f
mp
217
9
ff

221
mf
226
rit.
mp
rit.
230 a tempo
a tempo
mf
mf
Sfz
L.H.
Ped.
Ped.
Ped.
S.P.

233
pp
mp
p
(s.P.)
236
mp
mp
240
espr.
mf
p
mp

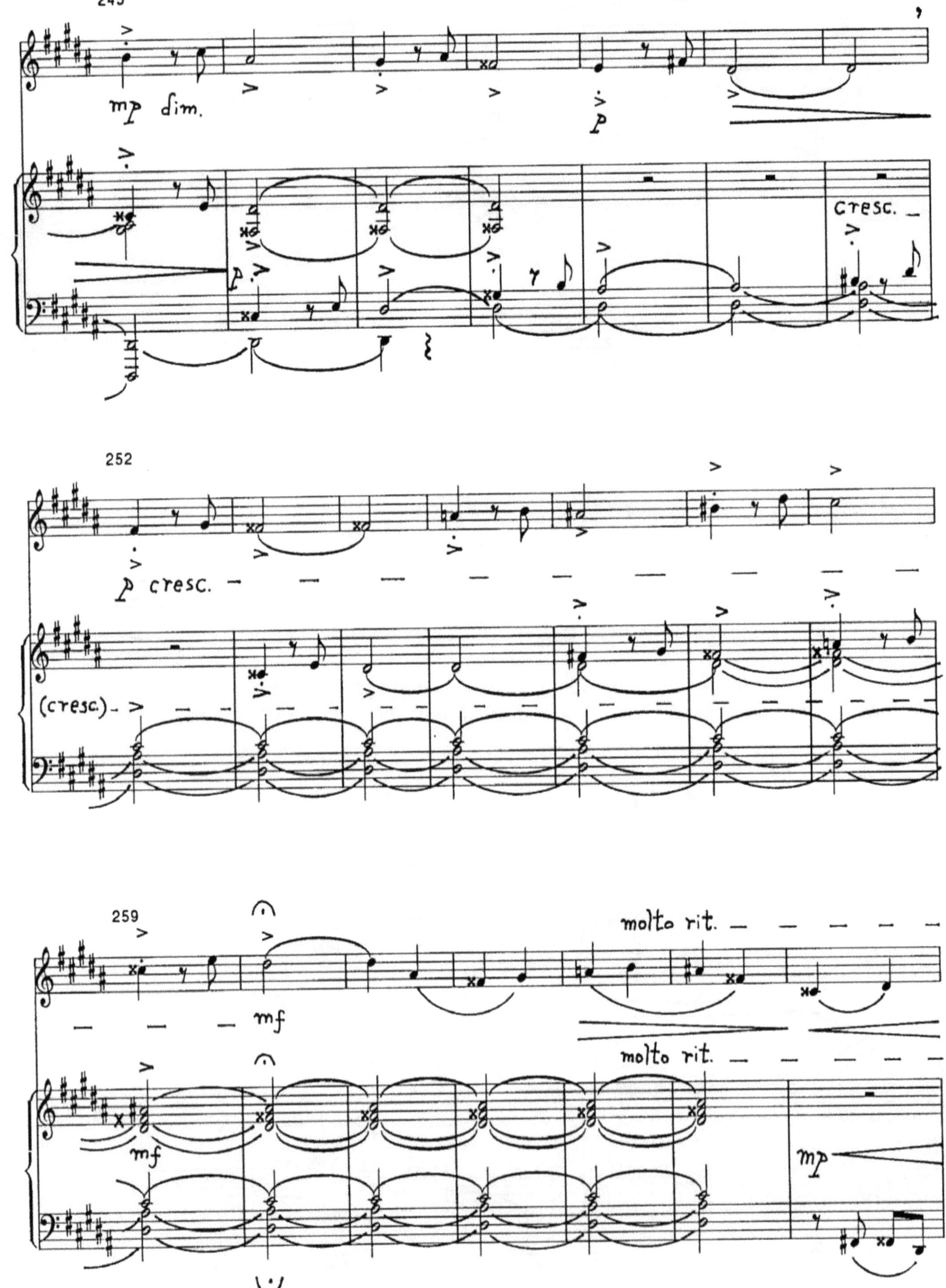
245
mp dim.
p
cresc.
252
p cresc.
(cresc.)
259
mf
molto rit.
mf
molto rit.
mp

266
mp
ppp
p
Sfz
Tempo 1
271
5
pp
p
Tempo 1
pp
276

283
PP
P
PP
Ped.
288
6
mp
mf
mp
mp
Ped.
292
6
mf
f
mf
mp

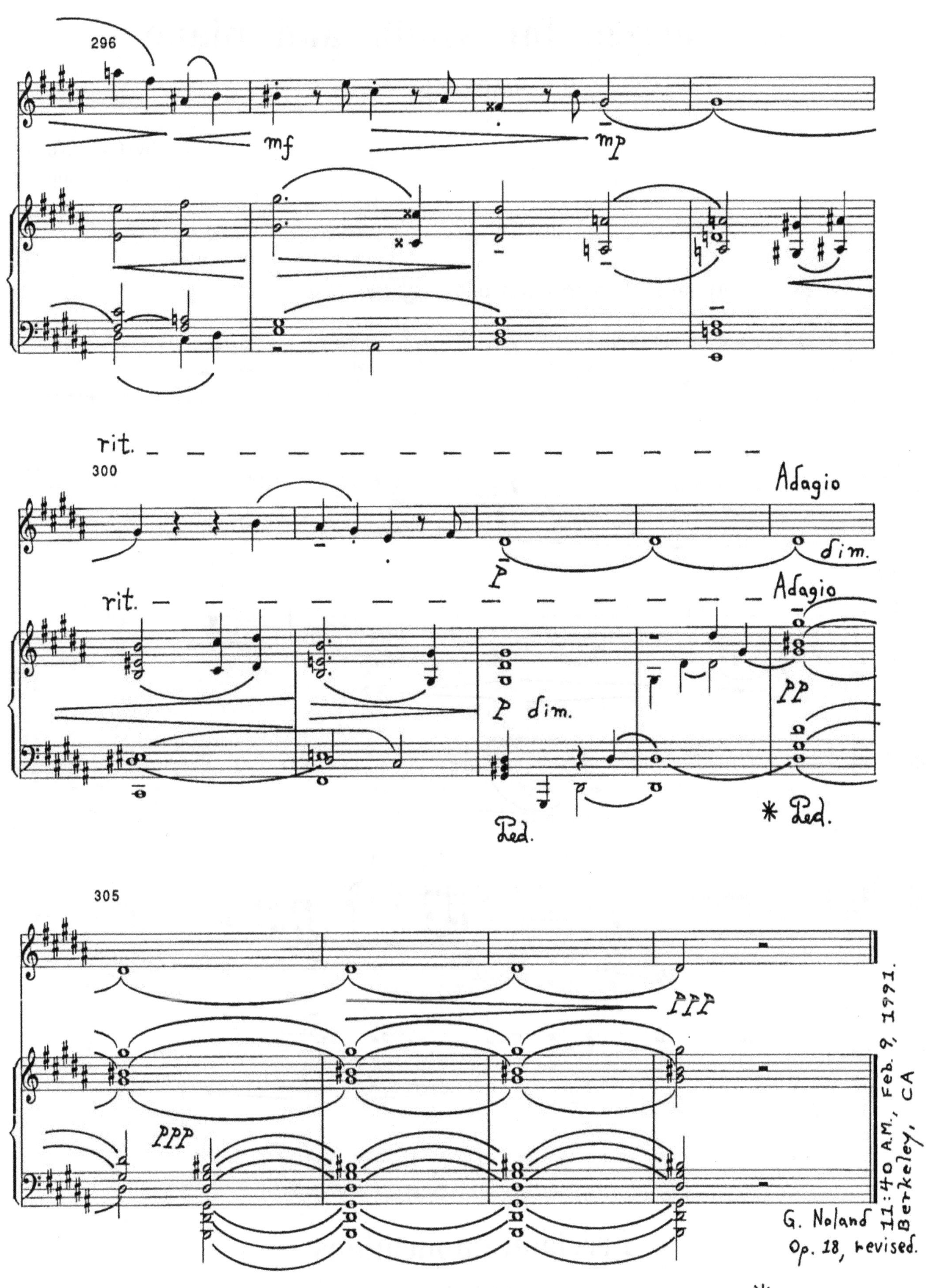
296
mf
mp
rit.
300
Adagio
p
dim.
rit.
Adagio
p dim.
pp
Ped.
* Ped.
305
ppp
ppp
11:40 A.M., Feb. 9, 1991.
Berkeley, CA
G. Noland
Op. 18, revised.
*

Intermezzo for violin and piano

violin part

by Gary Noland
op. 18

Freeland Publications

FP 21

36
mp
mf
f
40
mp
mf
rit.
45
a tempo
mp
mf
51
dolce
mp
mf
55
7
mp
p
60
mp
6
64
mf
67
6
f
3
3
3
6
mf
71
5
75
6
f
p cresc.

79
(cresc.)
f
poco dim.
85
mf
mp
91
(poco dim.)
97
4
(poco dim.)
6
pp
111
4
2
Pizz.
p
arco
poco rit.
Ländlich
(rustic)
poco meno mosso
121
mp
127
1
pp
132
mp
135
mf
139
2

144
p
mf
148
151
154
157
159
mf
mp
162
mf
f
166
mf
170
f
mf

172
f
mf
175
f
178
mf
182
f
ff
186
mf
p
mf
189
3
191
p cresc.
194
(cresc.)
mf
197
ff
f

200
mp
cresc.
203
f
206
ff
f
212
mf
f
9
217
ff
mf
222
5
rit.
a tempo
227
mp
231
mf
234
1
PP
mp
espr.
238
3
3
mf

mp
dim.
P
P cresc.
molto rit.
mf
Tempo 1
mP
PPP
pp
5
p
PP
6
mp
mf
mp
6
mf
f
mf
Adagio
mp
rit.
p
dim.
ppp

GARY NOLAND

DOG DUO

for

viola & cello

Op. 66a

FREELAND PUBLICATIONS

FP97

Dog Duo

for viola and cello

22
Vla.
Vc.
mf
f
27
ff
mf
31
mp
35
p
39

45
Vla.
Vc.
mf
51
f
mf
56
p
61
ff
65

69
Vla.
Vc.
mp
f
p
mf
73
81
85
tr

Dog Duo

for viola and cello

viola part

Gary Noland, Op. 66a

44
mf
50
f
mf
55
p
61
mf
f
ff
65
mf
f
69
mp
p
mf
73
mp
mf
78
p
f
84
tr
mf

Dog Duo

for viola and cello

cello part

Gary Noland, Op. 66a

43
mf
49
f
mf
54
p
61
mf
f
ff
66
mf
f
70
mp
p
mf
75
mp
mf
80
p
f
84

Gary Noland

Fantasy in E Minor

for cello & piano

Op. 24

Freeland Publications

"Fantasy in E Minor"

for cello and piano

by Gary Noland, Op. 24
(1984, revised 1992)

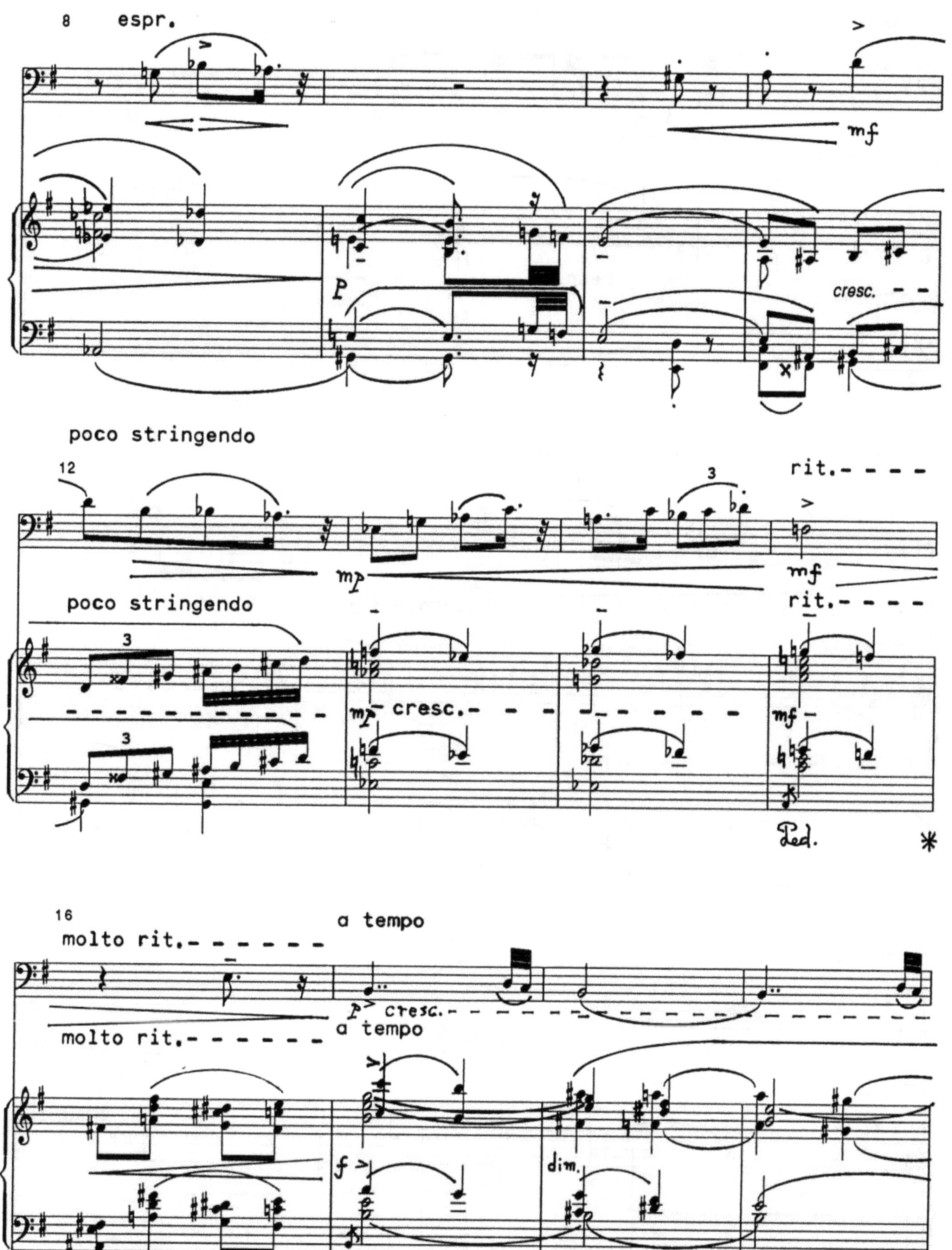
8
espr.
mf
p
cresc.
poco stringendo
12
3
rit.
mp
mf
poco stringendo
rit.
mp cresc.
mf
Ped.
16
molto rit.
a tempo
p cresc.
molto rit.
a tempo
f
dim.
Ped.

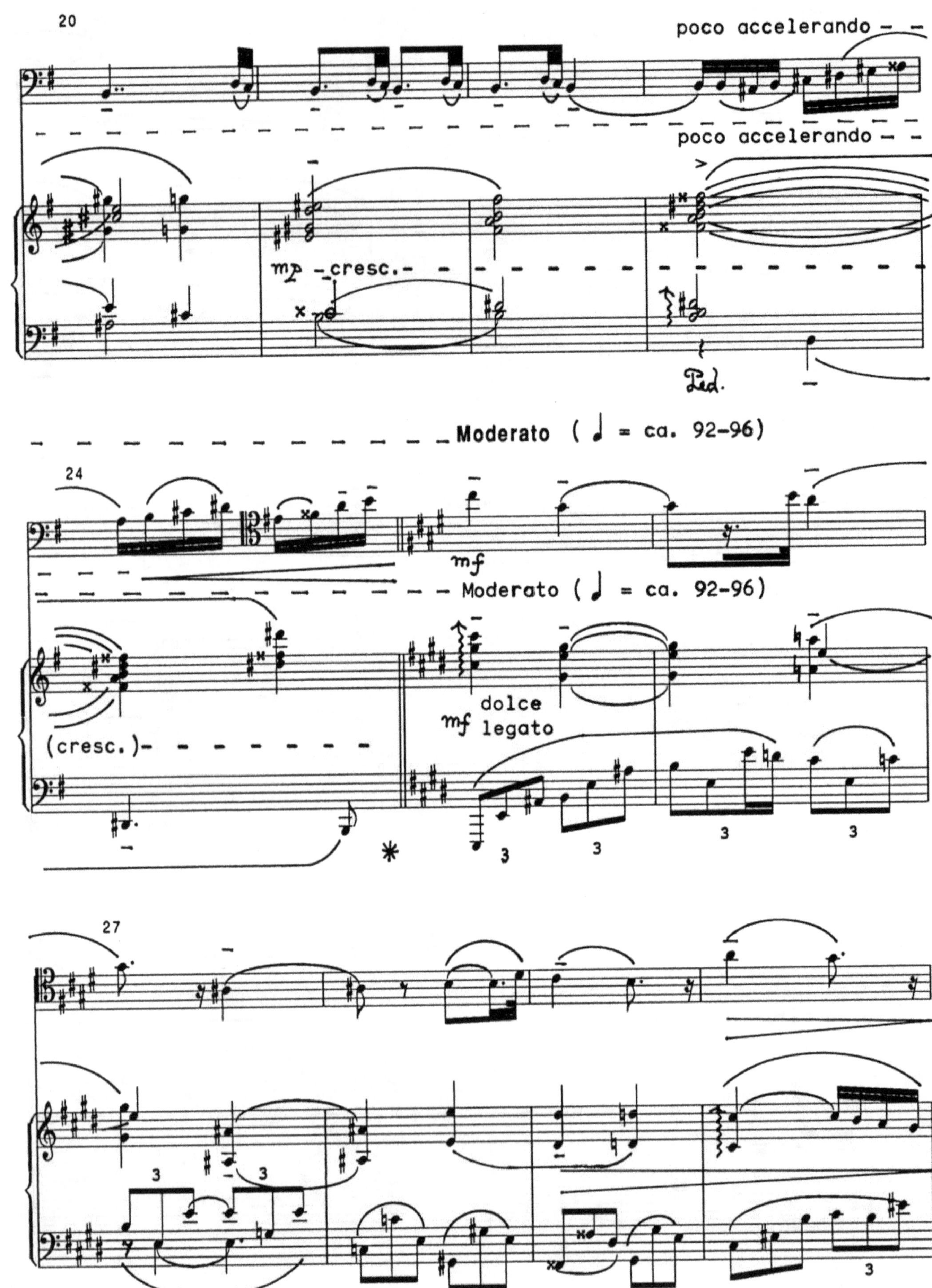
20
poco accelerando
poco accelerando
mp cresc.
Ped.
Moderato (= ca. 92-96)
24
mf
Moderato (= ca. 92-96)
dolce
mf legato
(cresc.)
27

31
mp
mf
mp
mf
35
mp
rit.
poco accel.
38
p cresc.
rit.
poco accel.
8va
mf
mp
mf
Ped.
*

a tempo
41
3
3
6
f
a tempo
8va
mp cresc.
3
44
mf
3
3
3
3
3
3
47
f
8va
f
ff
f
sfz
3
sfz
Ped.

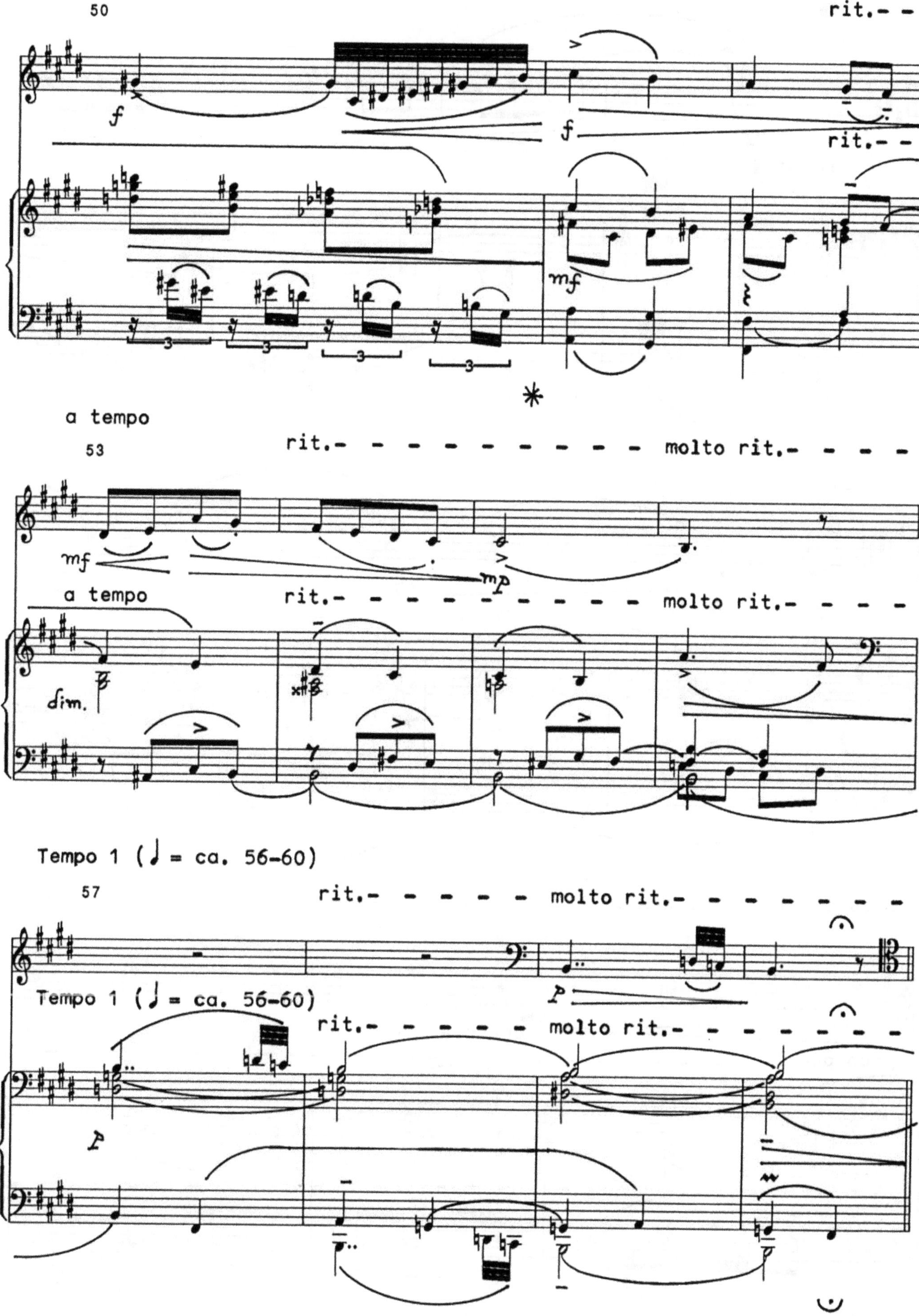

50
rit.- - -
f
f
rit.- - -
mf
a tempo
53
rit.- - - - - - - - - - - - - molto rit.- - - - -
mf
mp
a tempo
rit.- - - - - - - - - - - - - molto rit.- - - - -
dim.
Tempo 1 (♩ = ca. 56-60)
57
rit.- - - - - - molto rit.- - - - - - - - -
p
Tempo 1 (♩ = ca. 56-60)
rit.- - - - - - molto rit.- - - - - - - - -
p

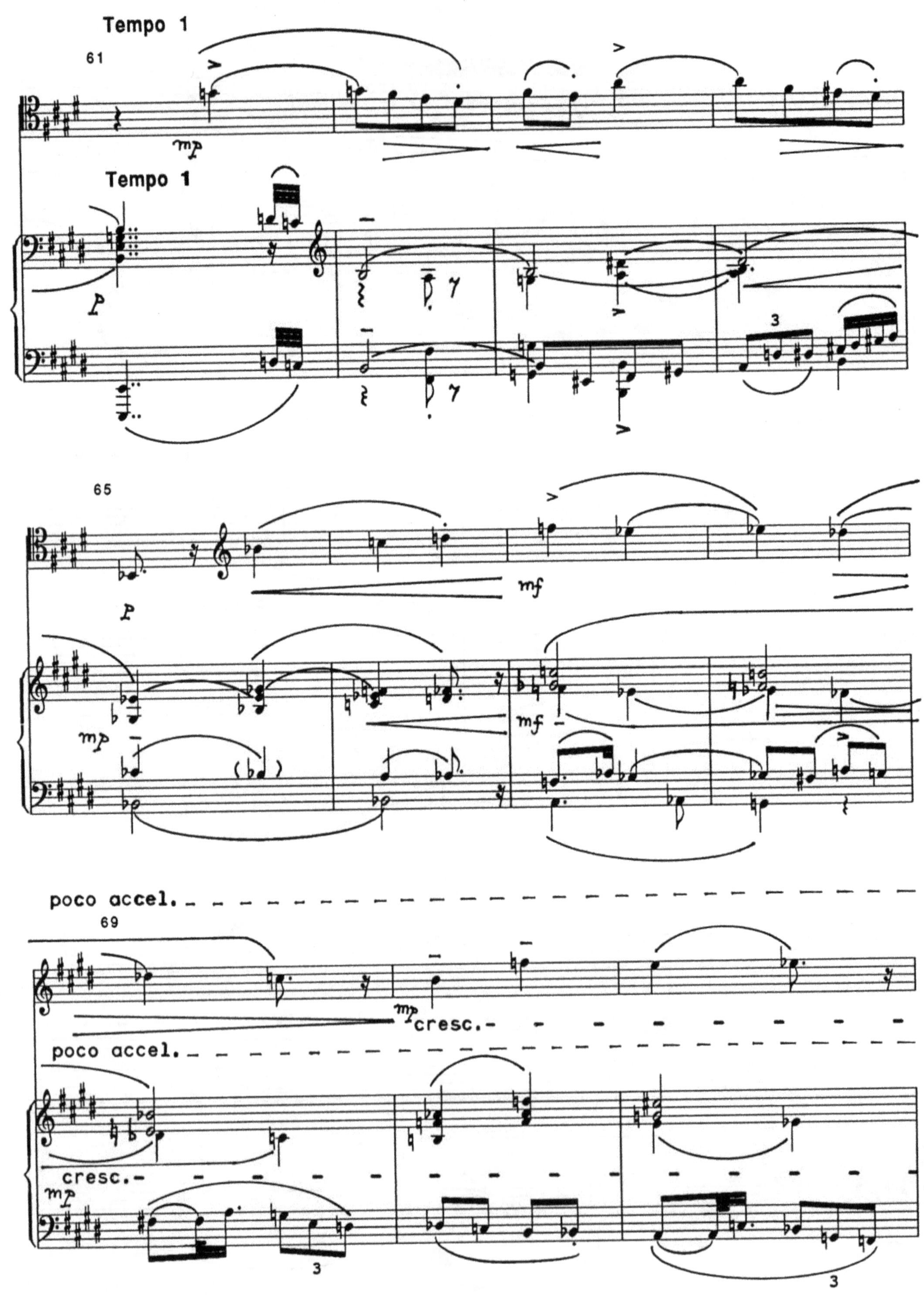
Tempo 1
61
mp
Tempo 1
p
3
65
p
mf
mp
mf
poco accel.
69
mp cresc.
poco accel.
cresc.
mp
3
3

rit.
meno mosso
72
f
meno mosso
rit.
(cresc.)
ff
75
f
mf
f
77
ff
ff

79
poco accel.
poco accel.
82
poco rit.
rit.
dim.
poco rit.
rit.
dim.
poco allegro
(𝅗𝅥 = ca. 112-120)
85
poco allegro
(𝅗𝅥 = ca. 112-120)

89
sul pont.
p

95
3

100

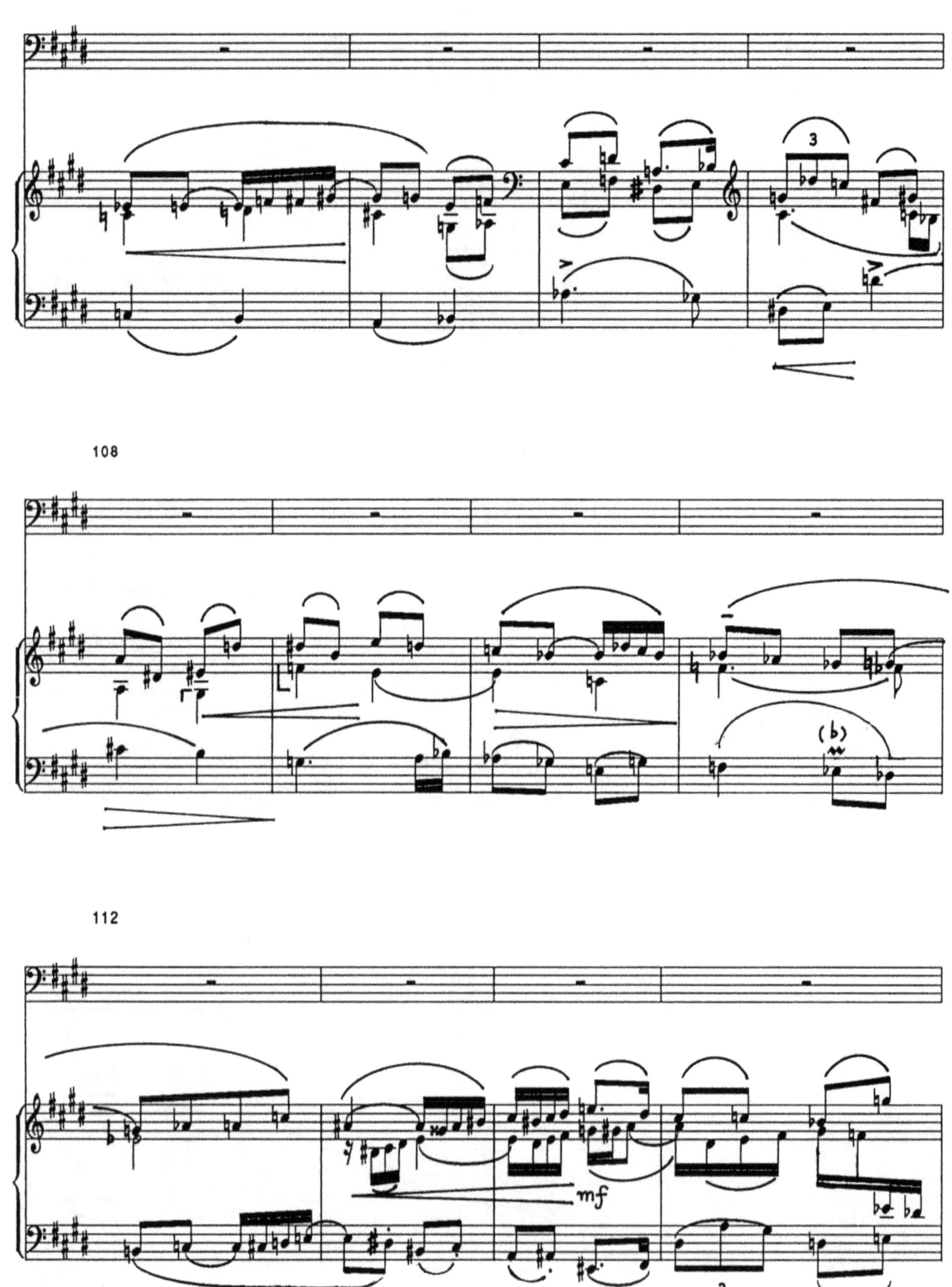
104
3
108
(♭)
112
mf
3

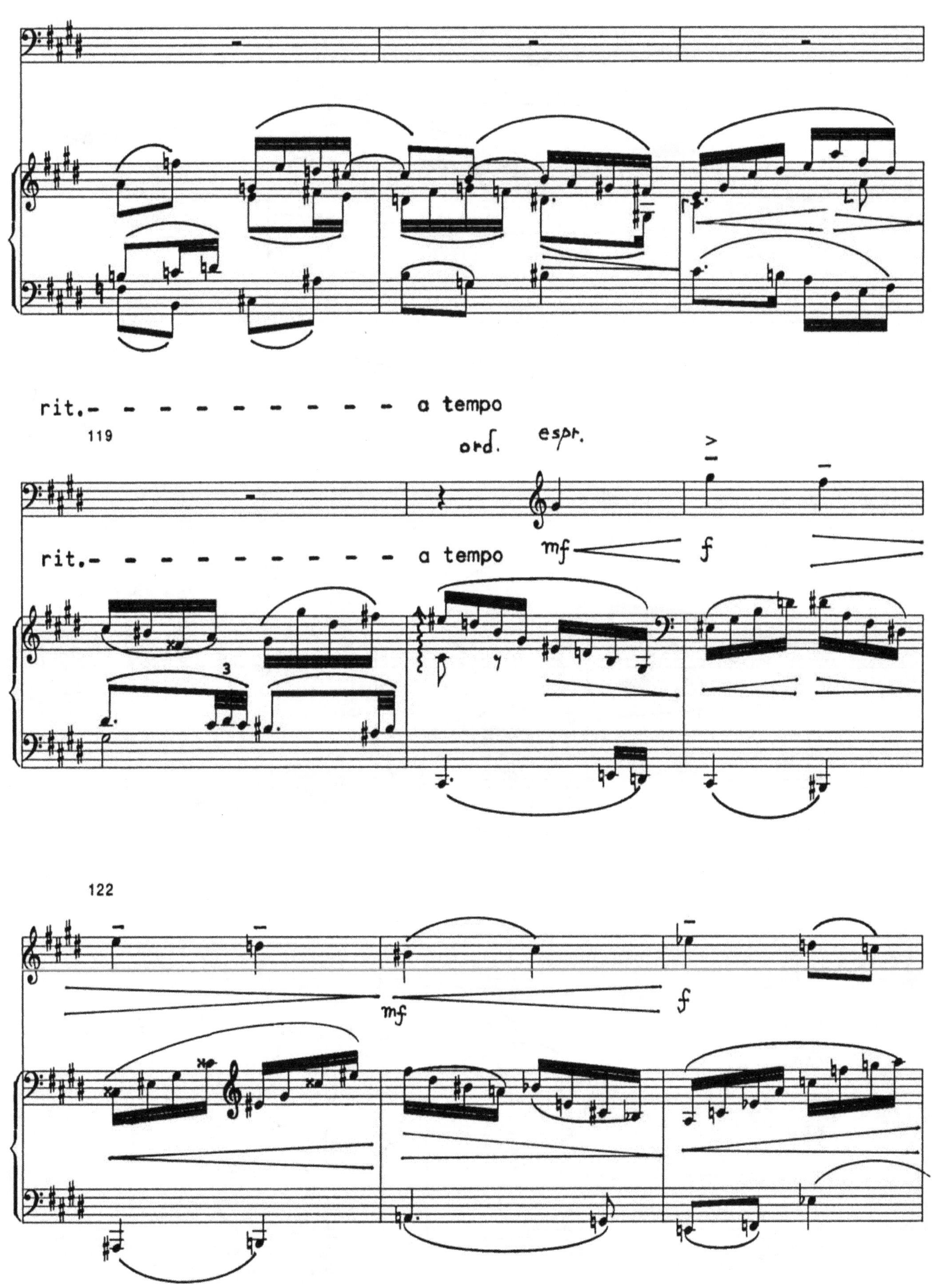
116
rit.- - - - - - - - - - - - - - a tempo
119
ord.
espr.
mf
f
rit.- - - - - - - - - - - - - - a tempo
3
122
mf
f

125
f
mf
f
mf
128
mp
(♮)
f
132
mf
mf
f
f

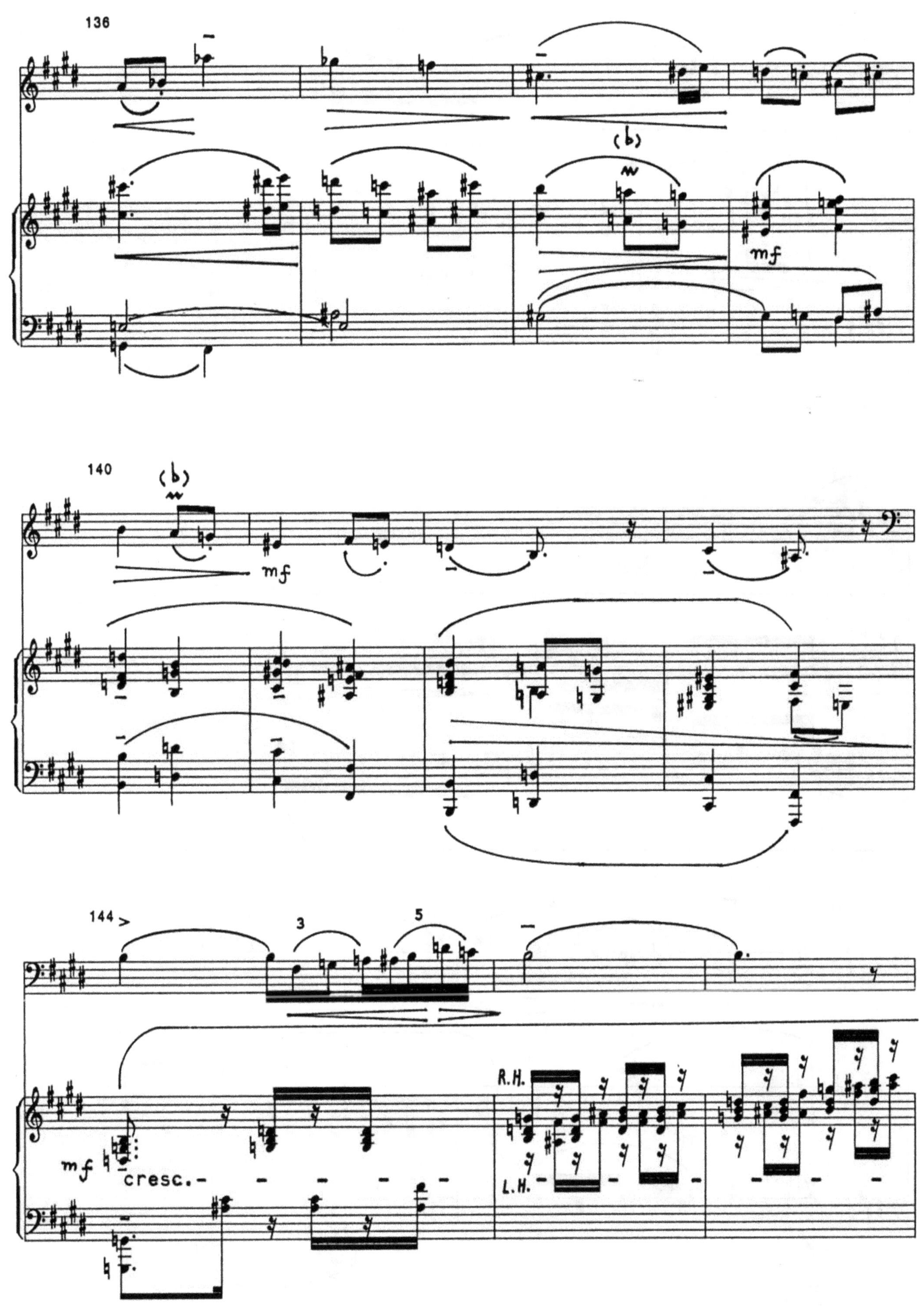

136
(♭)
mf
140
(♭)
mf
144
3
5
R.H.
L.H.
mf
cresc.

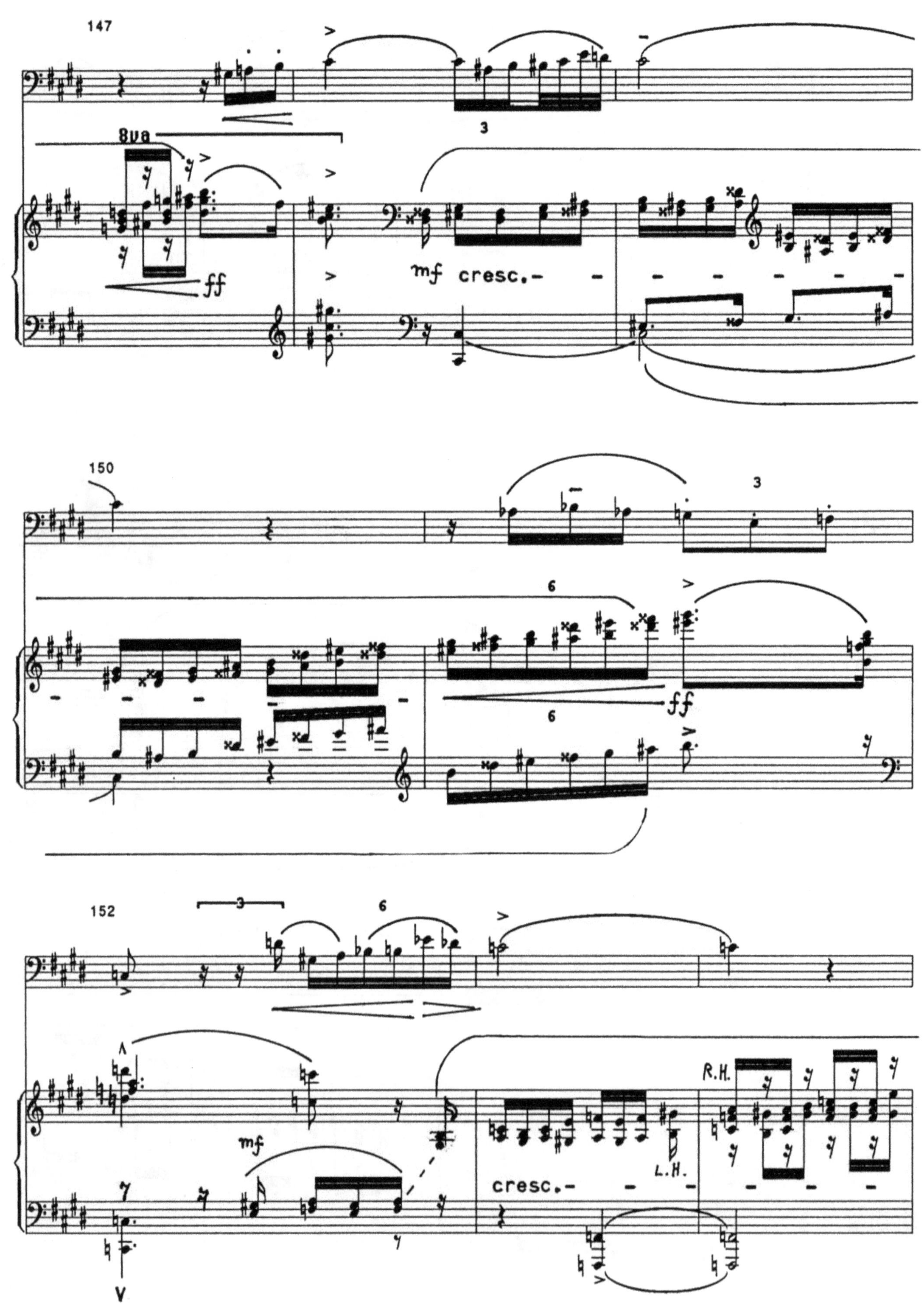
147
8va
ff
mf cresc.-
3
150
6
3
152
mf
6
cresc.-
L.H.
R.H.

155
8va
Ped.
*Ped.
*
158
161

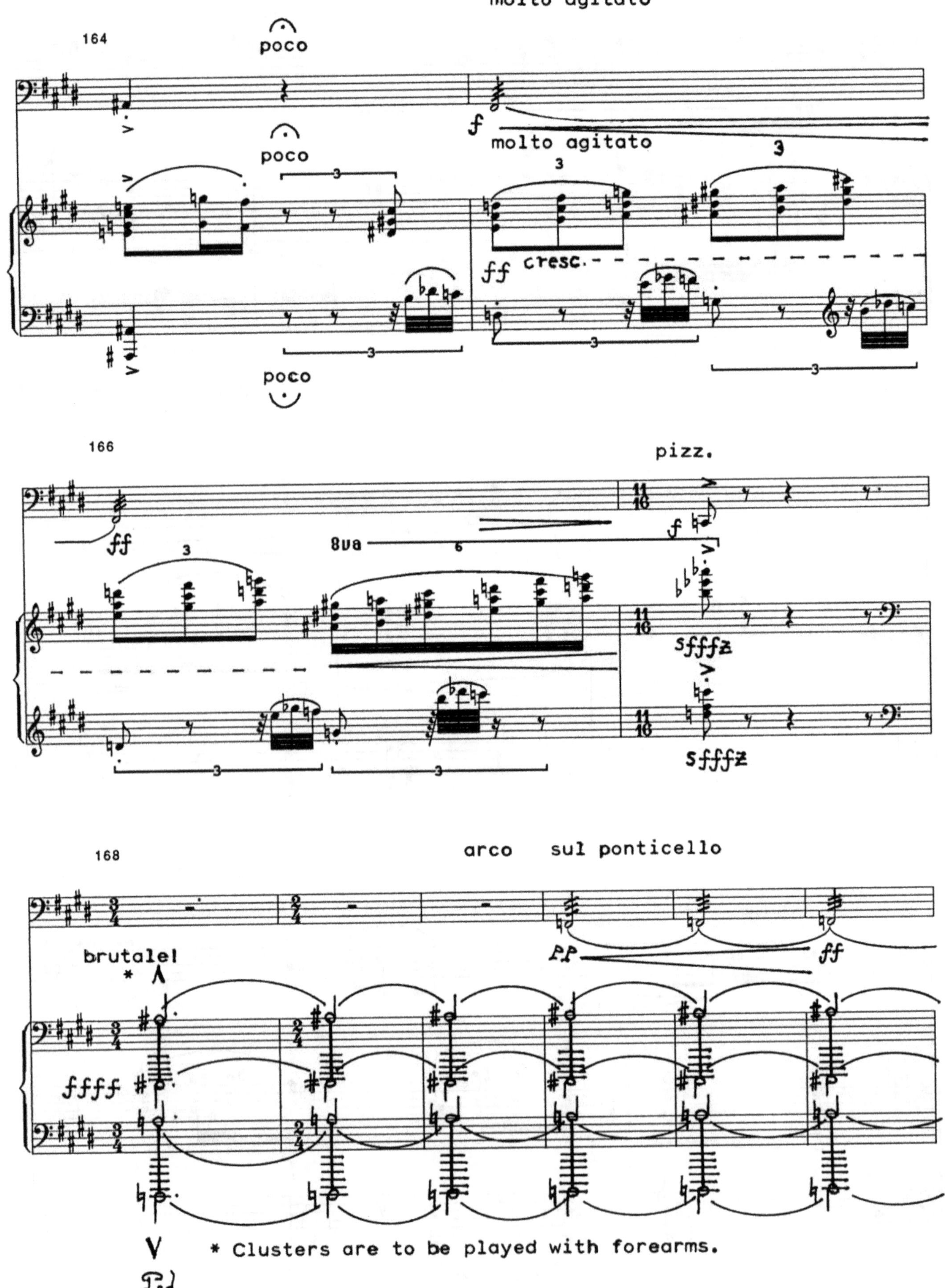
molto agitato
164
poco
poco
molto agitato
cresc.
poco
166
pizz.
8va
sfffz
sfffz
168
arco sul ponticello
brutale!
ffff
* Clusters are to be played with forearms.
Ped.

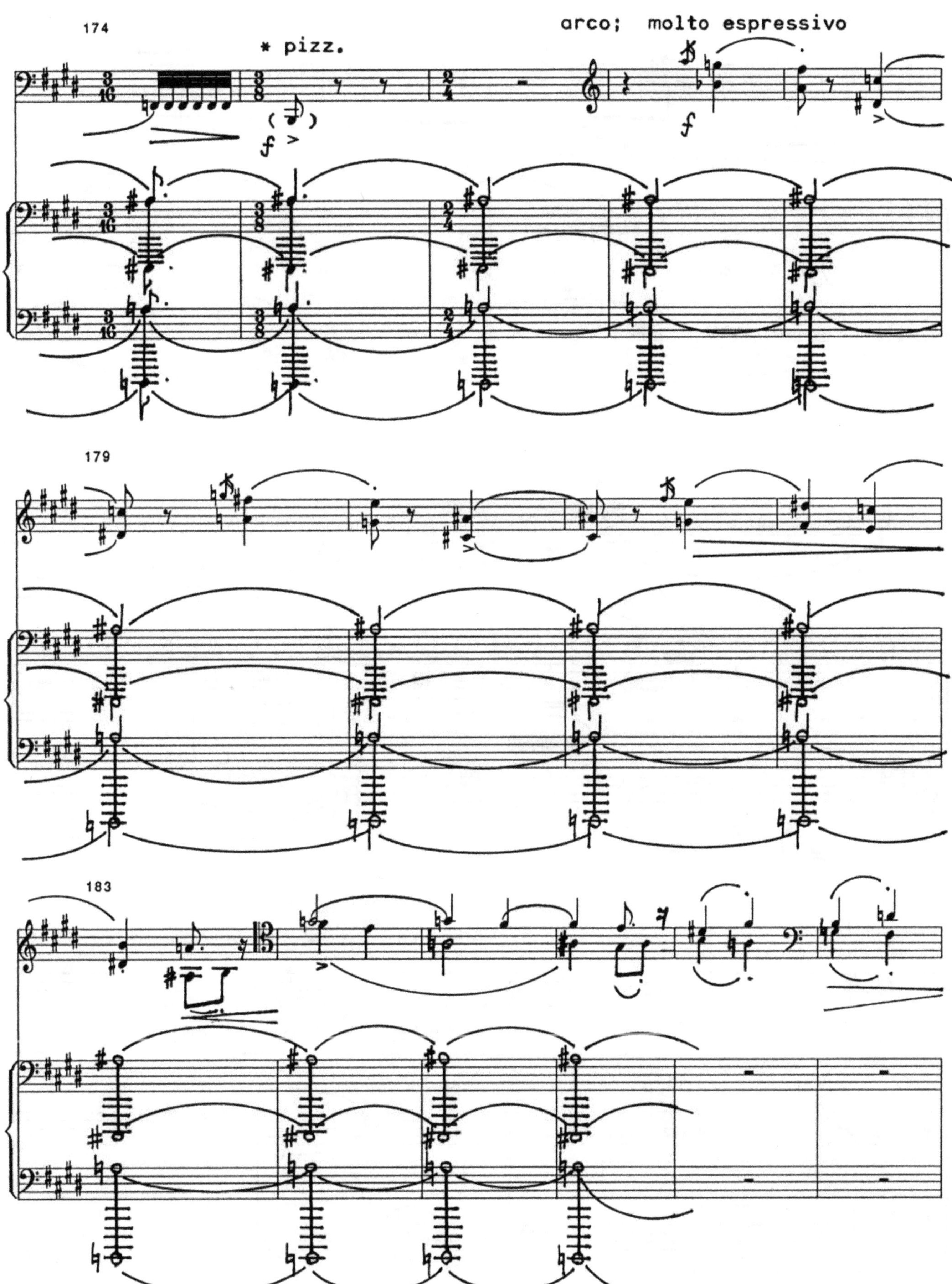

*Scordatura. If possible, the C-string should be tuned to B; otherwise two instruments may be utilized (or, if necessary, two cellists).

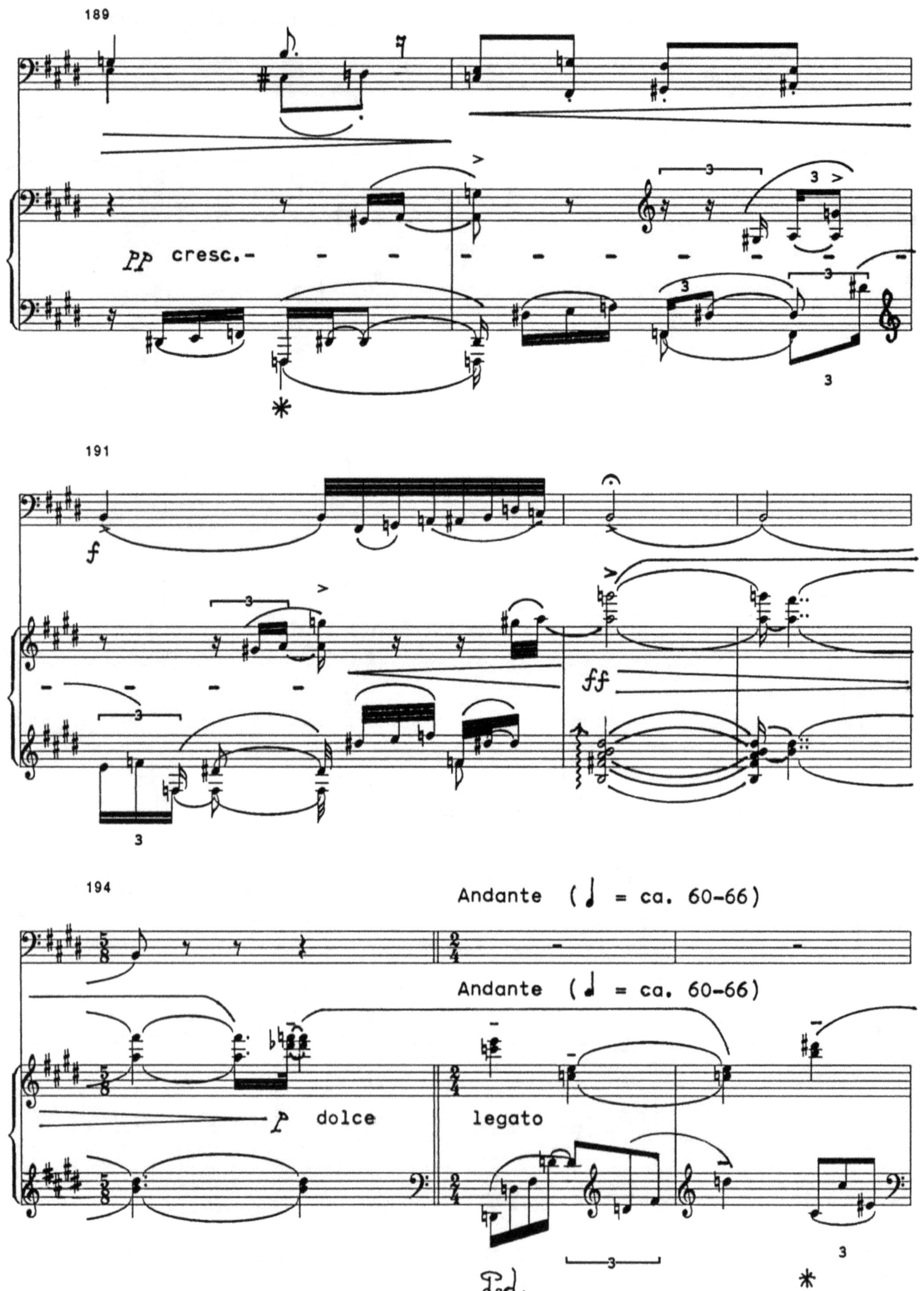
189
pp cresc.-
191
f
ff
194
Andante (♩ = ca. 60-66)
Andante (♩ = ca. 60-66)
p dolce
legato
Ped.

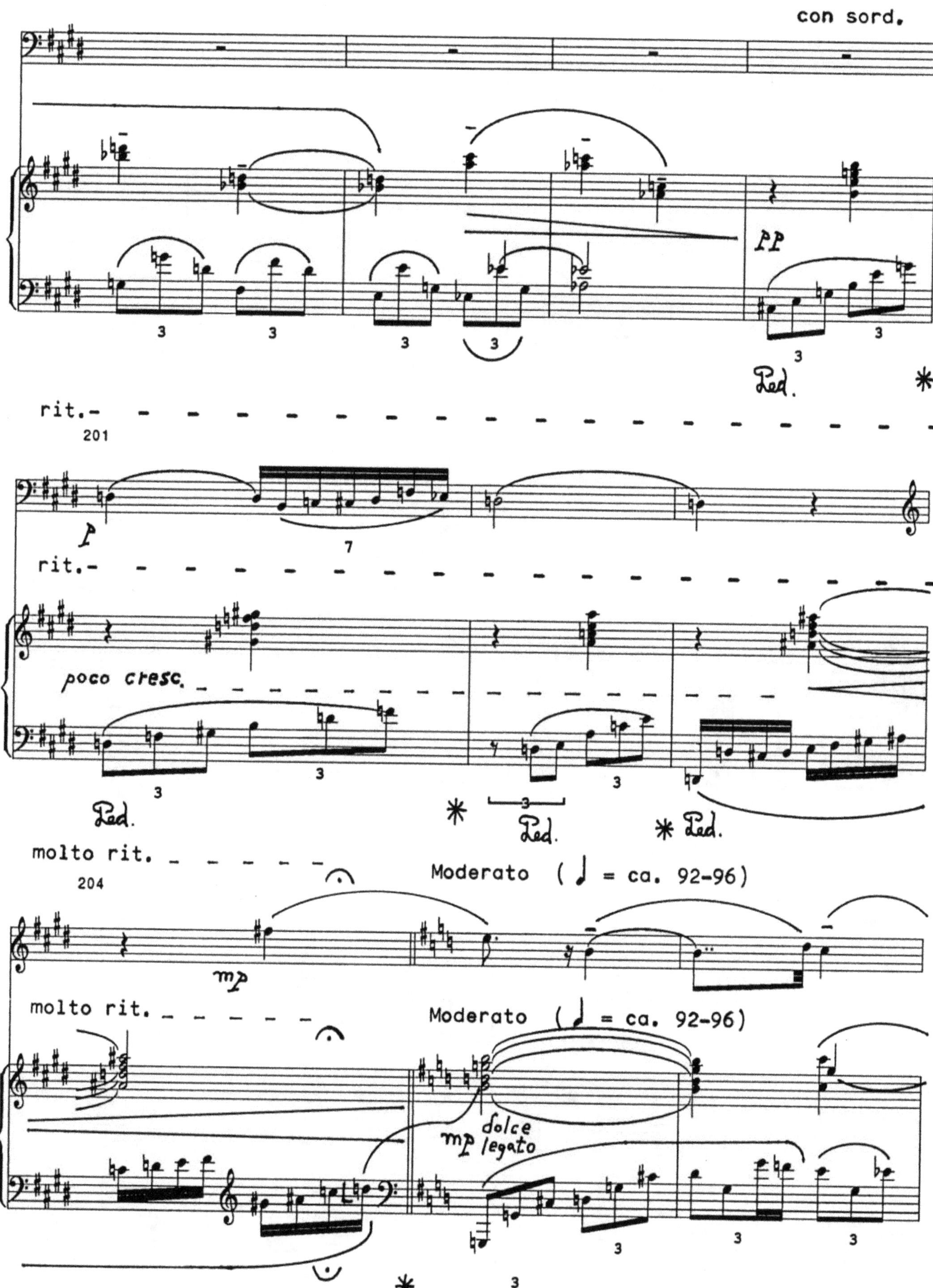
197
con sord.
PP
Ped.
rit.
201
P
7
rit.
poco cresc.
Ped.
Ped.
Ped.
molto rit.
204
Moderato (= ca. 92-96)
mp
molto rit.
Moderato (= ca. 92-96)
dolce
mp legato

207
Ped.
212
215

219
mp cresc.
223
senza sord.
mf
f
cresc.
226
f
8va
ff

229
8va
sfz
sfz
mf
232
rit.
mf
rit.
8va
a tempo
235
rit.
f
mf
a tempo
8va
sfz
mp
rit.

- - - - - - - - - - - a tempo
238
f
- f - - - - - - - - - - a tempo
8va
sfz
mf
mp
rit. - - - - - - - - - a tempo
242
rit. - - - - - - - a tempo
8va
mf
sfz
245
mp
rit. - - - - - a tempo
f
mf
rit. - - - 8va - a tempo
f
sfz

249
mp
mf
dolce
253
dolce
257
mp
mp
mp
mf

261
mf
f
3
3
264
molto rit.
a tempo
f
8va
molto rit.
a tempo
sfz
mf
f
rit.
a tempo
267
mf
rit.
a tempo
8va
f
mp
mf
f
sfz

271
mf
f
mp
mf
275
(♮)
mf
f
mp
cresc.
278
f
f
f

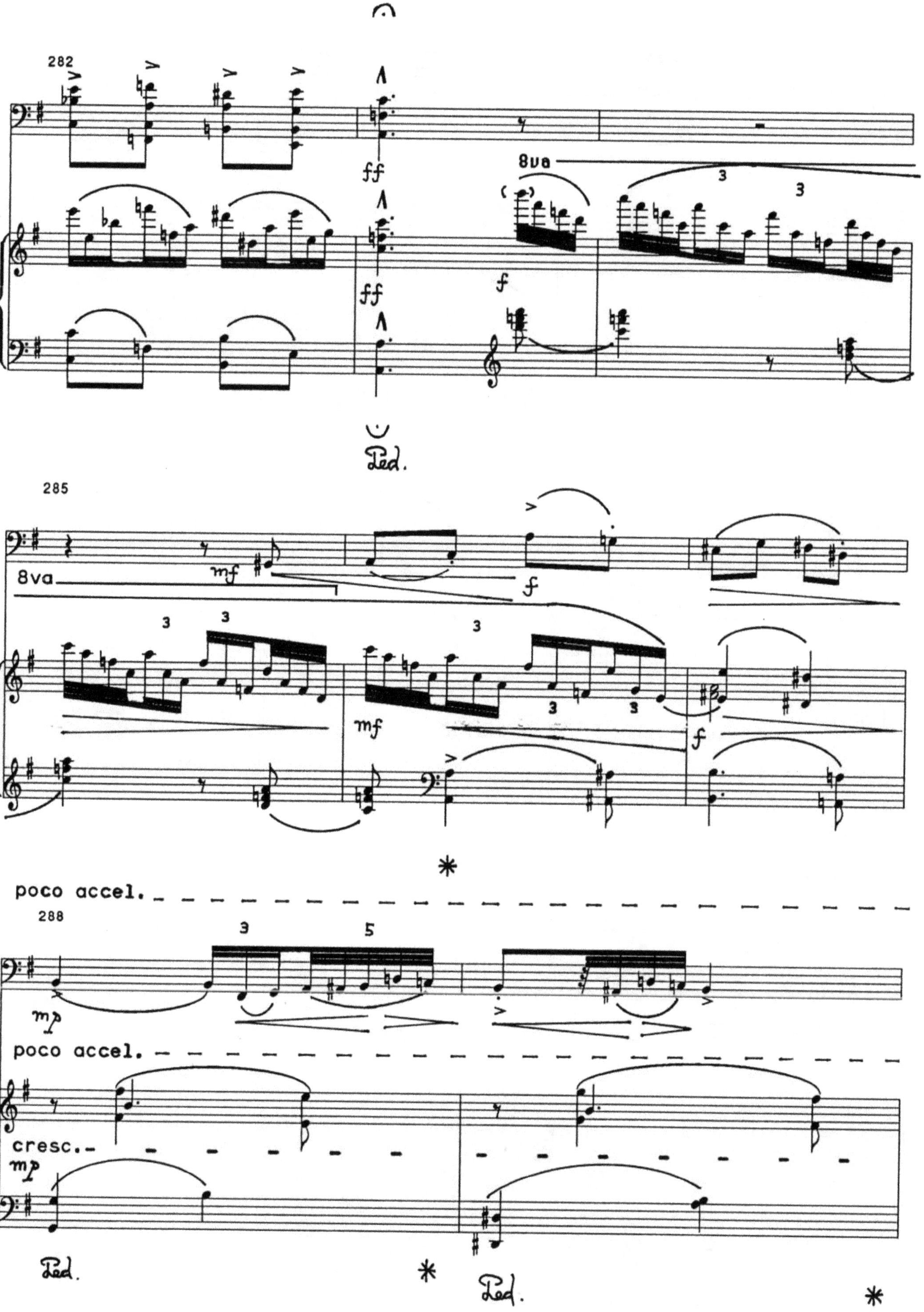

282

ff

8va

ff

f

Ped.

285

mf

8va

f

mf

f

poco accel.

288

mp

poco accel.

cresc.

mp

Ped.

Ped.

290
mf
(cresc.)
Ped.
*
293
rit.
a tempo
cresc.
f
mf
mp
296
cresc.

300
rit. - - - a tempo
f
mf
mp
rit. - - - a tempo
f
f
mp cresc. poco a poco
f
303
allargando
mf
allargando
f
307
meno mosso (= ca. 76-80)
mf
meno mosso (= ca. 76-80)
8va
ff

311
mp
mf
f
315
mp
mf
f
Ped.
*
319
Pizz.
mp
mf
p

322
arco
Pizz.
f
mp
mf
p
325
arco
a tempo
f
mf
a tempo
f
mf dim.
rit.- - - - - - - a tempo
328
mp
p cresc.
8va
rit.- - - - - - - a tempo
mp
mf
p

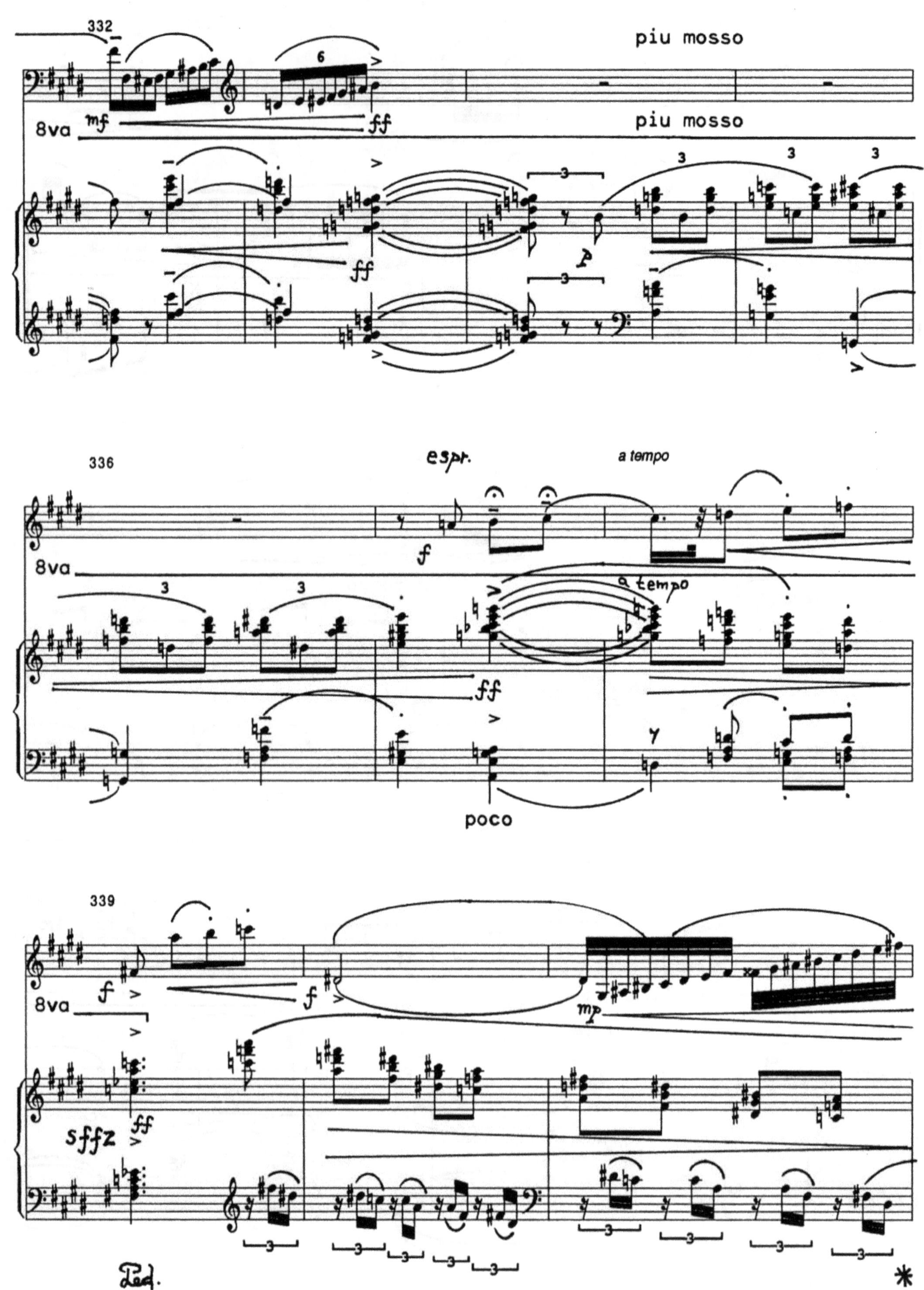
332
piu mosso
mf
ff
8va
piu mosso
p
336
espr.
a tempo
f
8va
a tempo
ff
poco
339
f
8va
f
mp
sffz
ff
Ped.

ritardando
molto espressivo
342
f
ritardando
8va
mp
f
f
346
a tempo
rit.
mf
a tempo
rit.
mp
mp
mf
mp
a tempo
350
a tempo
mp
cresc.
3
5
f
3
5

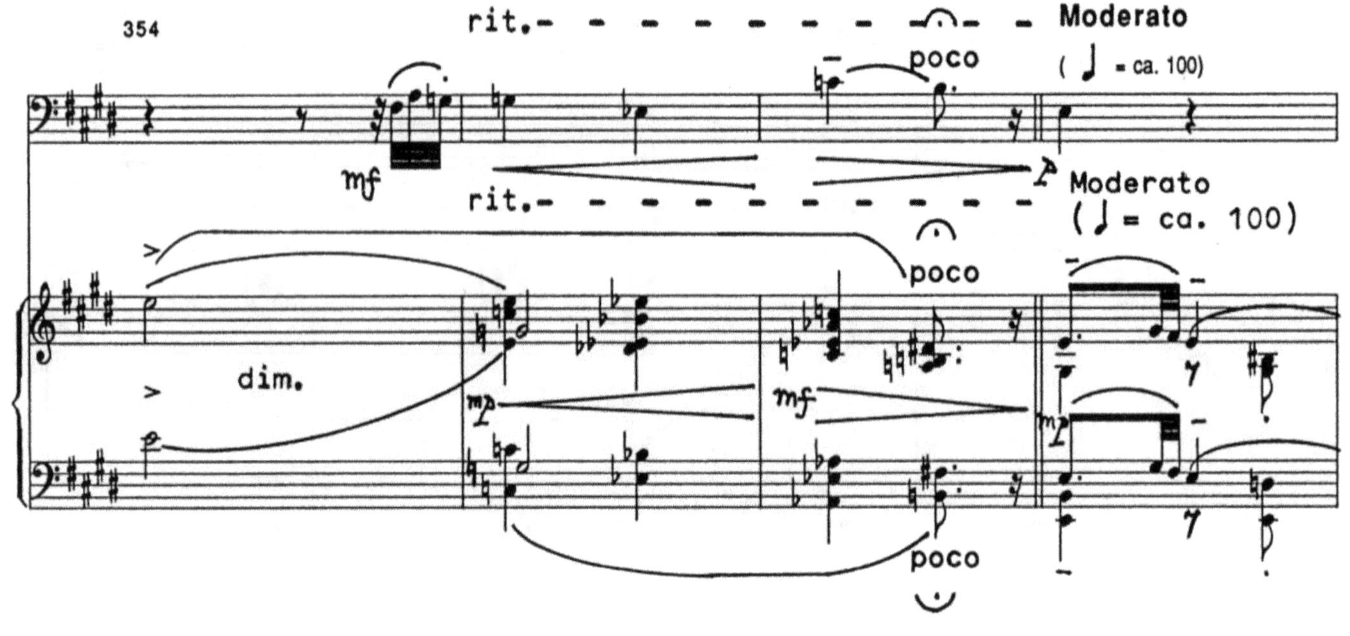
354
rit.
poco
Moderato
(♩ = ca. 100)
mf
rit.
Moderato
(♩ = ca. 100)
poco
dim.
mp
mf
mp
poco

358
mp
cresc.

360
mf
f
mf

363
mf
cresc.
ff
365
f
p
rit.
molto rit.
368
espr.
cresc.
rit.
molto rit.
p
cresc.
Ped.
* Ped.
*

a tempo
372
f
mf
dim.
a tempo
8va
legato
mp
3
377
mp
mf
dim.
380
dolce
p

rit. - - - - - - - - - - - - - - molto rit. - - -
383
mf
mp
molto rit. - - -
rit. - - - - - - - - - - - - - -
mp
mf
Tempo 1 (𝅗𝅥 = ca. 56-60)
387
molto rit.- - -
Tempo 1 (𝅗𝅥 = ca. 56-60)
molto rit.- - -
mp dim.
a tempo
391
mp
3
a tempo
p
mp
mp
mf

395
espr.
mf
mp
mf
399
poco stringendo
poco stringendo
mp
403
rit.
mf cresc.
f
f
rit.
Ped.
Ped.

rit.
a tempo
406
mf a tempo
8va
rit.
ff
dim.
Ped.
409
mp
cresc.
8va
mp
412
8va
f
f

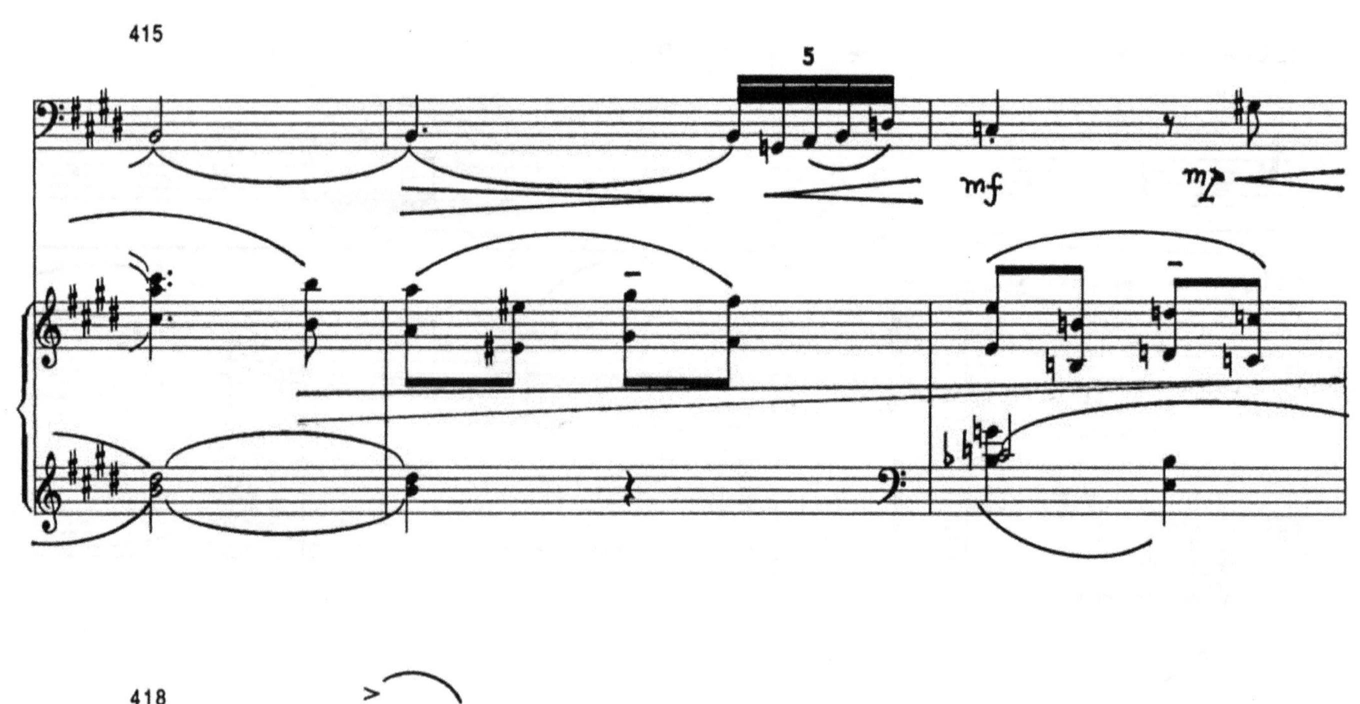
415
5
mf
mp

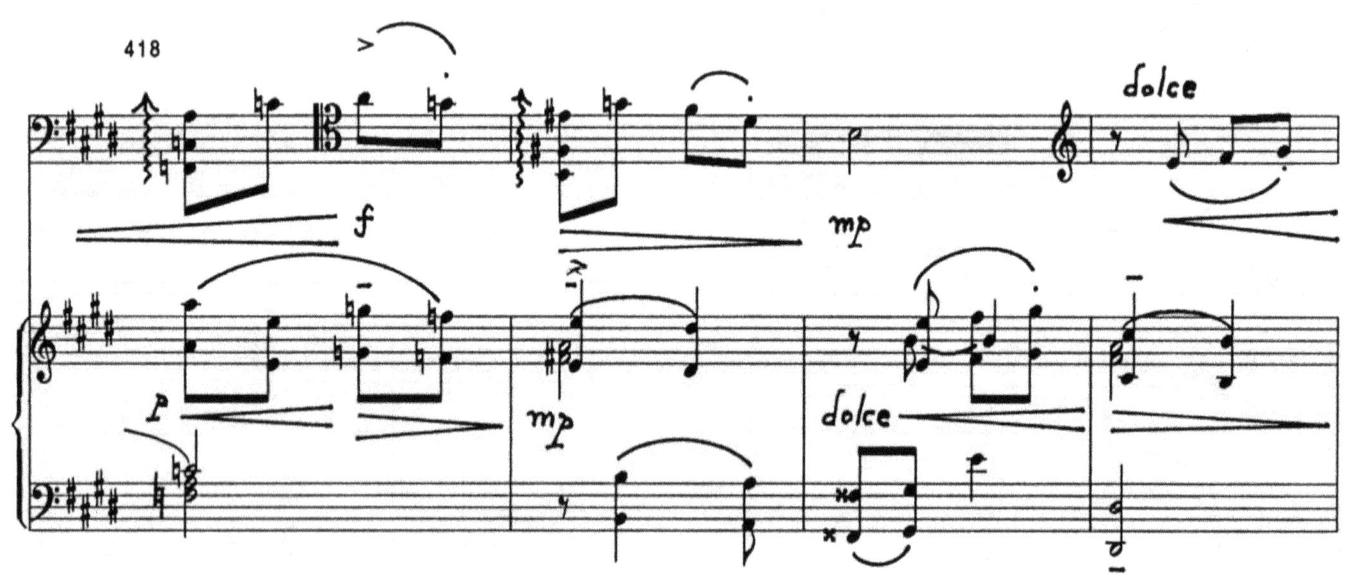
418
dolce
f
mp
p
mp
dolce

422
mf
mp
mf
mp

427
mp
mf
mf
mp
mf
mf
f
3
rit.
431
rit.
8va
3
3
mf
a tempo
434
f
a tempo
8va
sfz
f

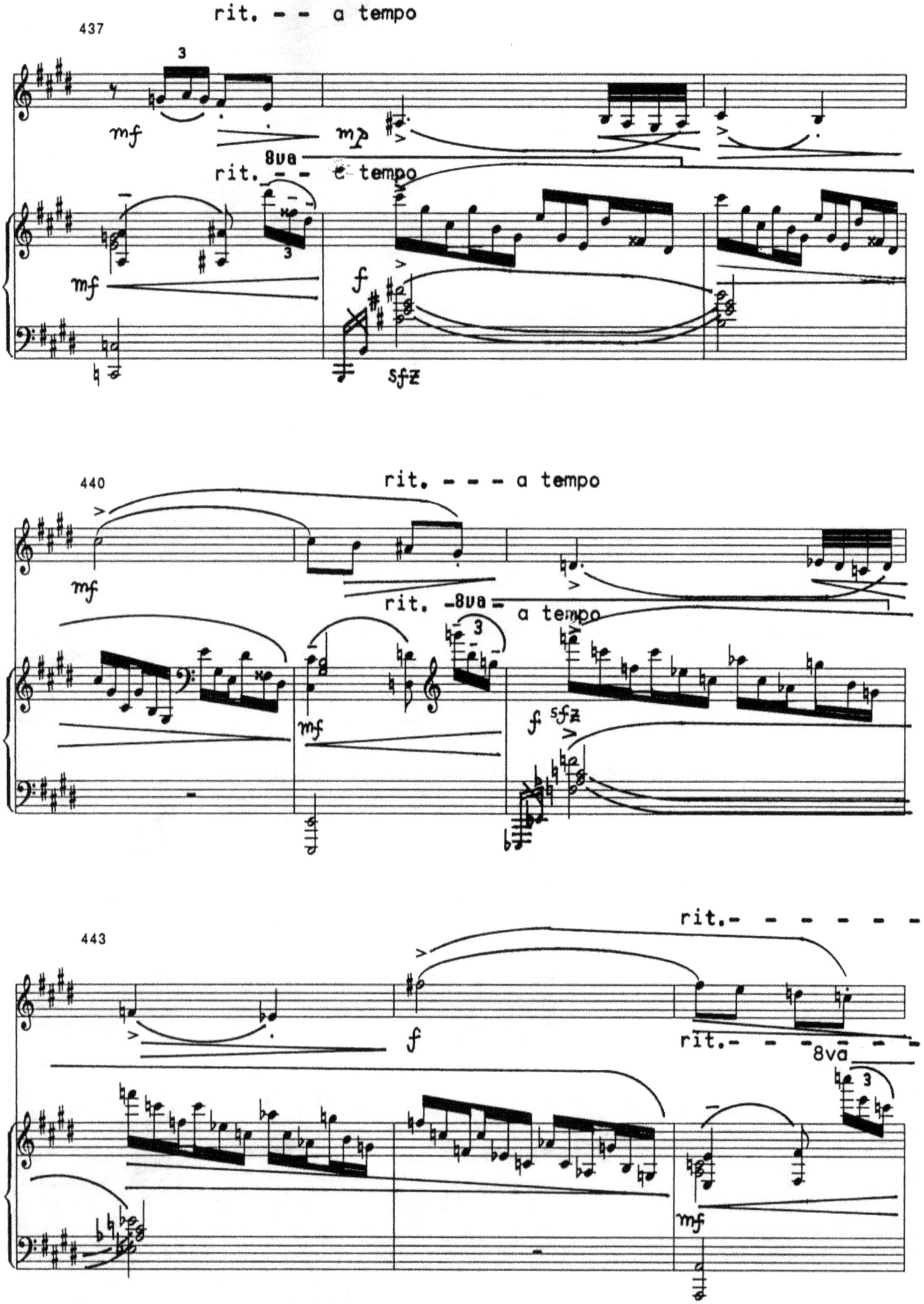

437

rit. - - a tempo

3

mf

mp

8va

rit. - - a tempo

3

mf

f

sfz

440

rit. - - - a tempo

mf

rit. 8va a tempo

3

mf

f

sfz

a tempo
446
8va
a tempo
ff
ff
Ped.
449
3
3
3
3
3
3
mf
p
* Ped.
*
452
8va
mf
ff
5
2 1
5 3 2 1
7
7
7
7

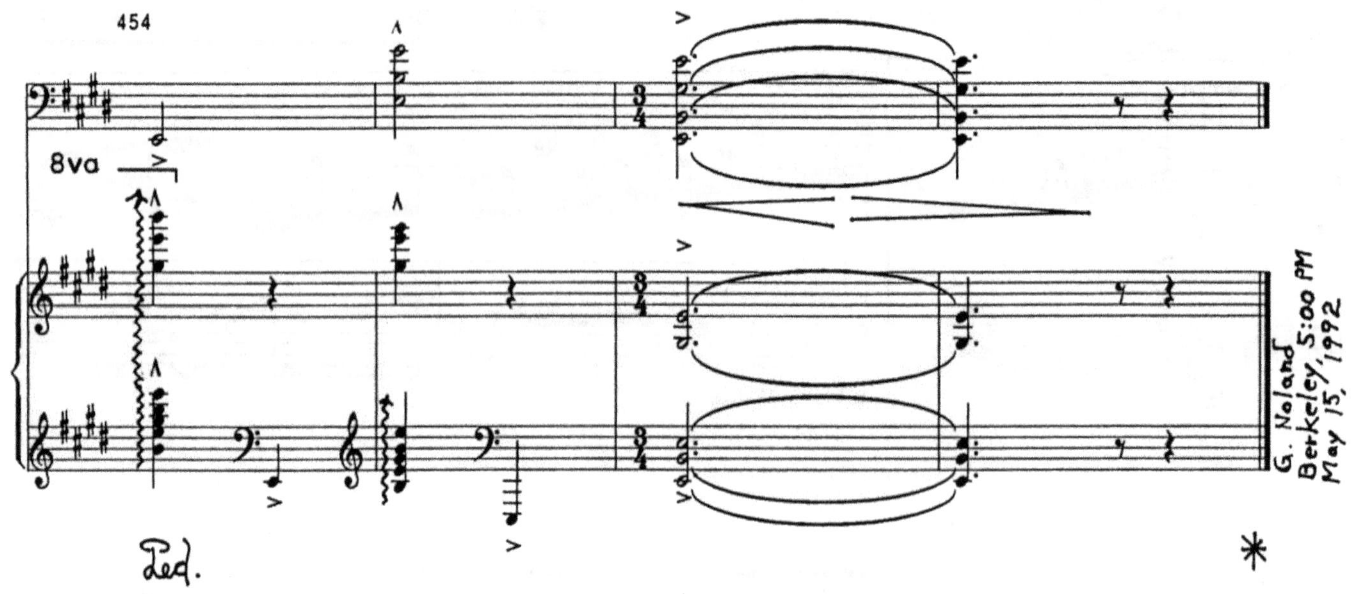
454
8va
Ped.
G. Noland
Berkeley, 5:00 PM
May 15, 1992

"Fantasy in E Minor"

for cello and piano

by Gary Noland, op. 24
(1984, revised 1992)

rit.- - - - - - - - - - - poco accel.- a tempo
p cresc.
mf
rit.- - - a tempo rit.- - - - -
molto rit.- - - -
Tempo 1 rit.
(♩= ca. 56-60)
molto rit.
Tempo 1
poco accel.
mp cresc.
rit.
meno mosso
ff

79
poco accel.-
3
5
f
ff
poco rit.- - rit.-
poco allegro
(♩ = ca. 112-120)
82
dim.
mf
f
87
sul pont.
mp
p
92
25
piano
rit.
a tempo
120
ord.
espr.
mf
f
126
3
134
139
(♭)
144

*Scordatura. If possible, the C-string should be tuned to B; otherwise two instruments may be utilized (or, if necessary, two cellists).

Andante (♩= ca. 60-66)
con sord.
rit.
molto rit.
Moderato
(♩ = ca. 92-96)
senza sord.
rit.
a tempo
rit.
a tempo
rit.
a tempo

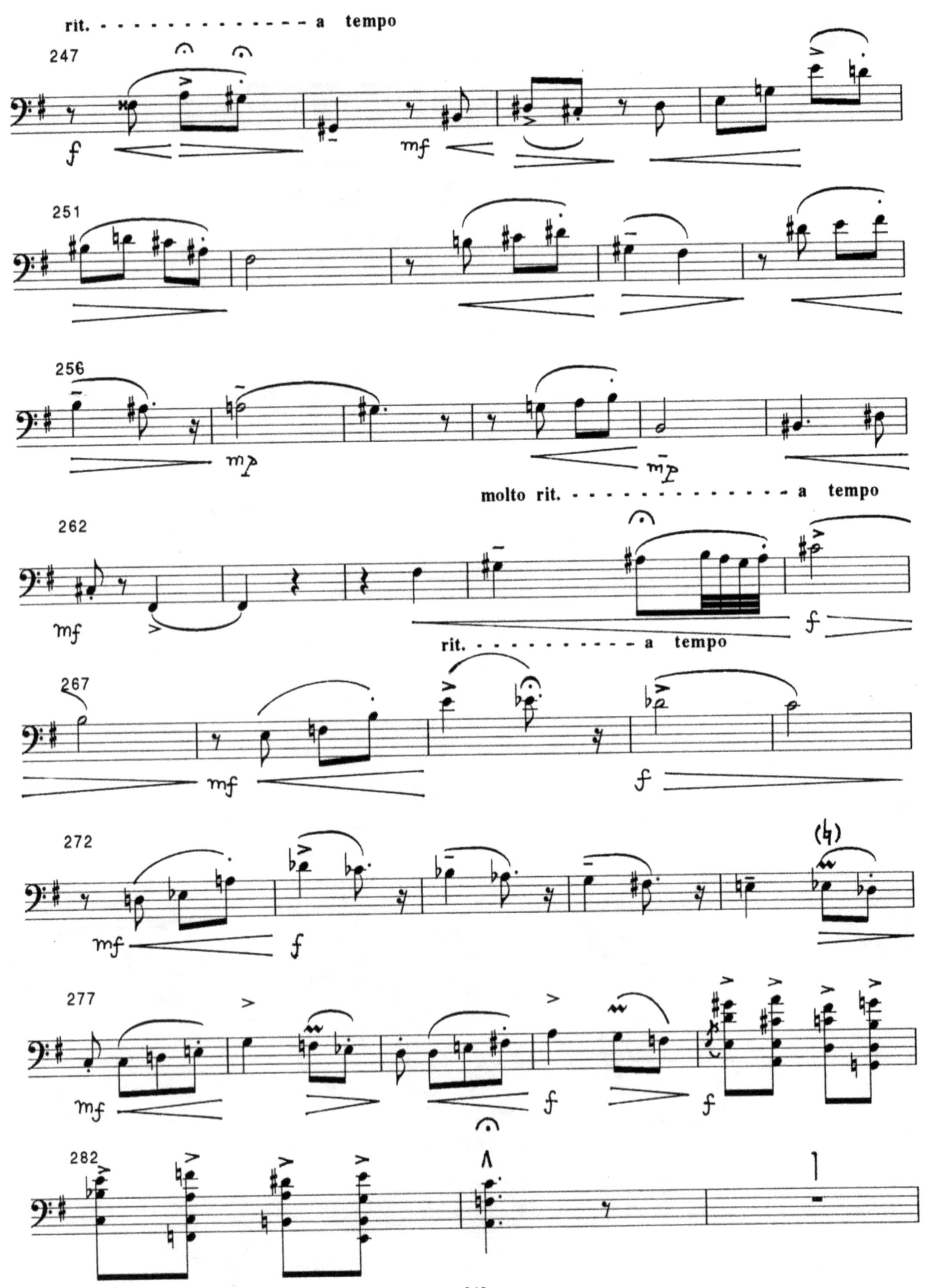
rit. - - - - - - - - - - - - - - a tempo
247
f
mf
251
256
mp
mp
molto rit. - - - - - - - - - - - - - - - - a tempo
262
mf
f
rit. - - - - - - - - - - - a tempo
267
mf
f
272
mf
f
277
mf
f
f
282

285
poco accel.
mf
f
mp
289
mf
292
cresc.
rit.
294
a tempo
f
mf
mp
mf
298
rit.
a tempo
f
f
301
mf
mp
mp
mf
allargando
306
f
meno mosso
(♩ = ca. 76-80)
mf
311
mp
f
mp
316
f
mp

Pizz.
arco
Pizz.
arco
a tempo
rit.
a tempo
cresc.
piu mosso
espr.
a tempo
ritardando
molto espressivo
a tempo
rit.
a tempo
rit.
poco
Moderato
(♩ = ca. 100)

364
rit.
molto rit.
368
cresc.
a tempo
372
dim.
377
dim.
dolce
380
rit.
molto rit.
Tempo 1
(♩ = ca. 56-60)
molto rit.
a tempo
385
393
398
espr.
poco stringendo
rit.
a tempo
404
408
cresc.

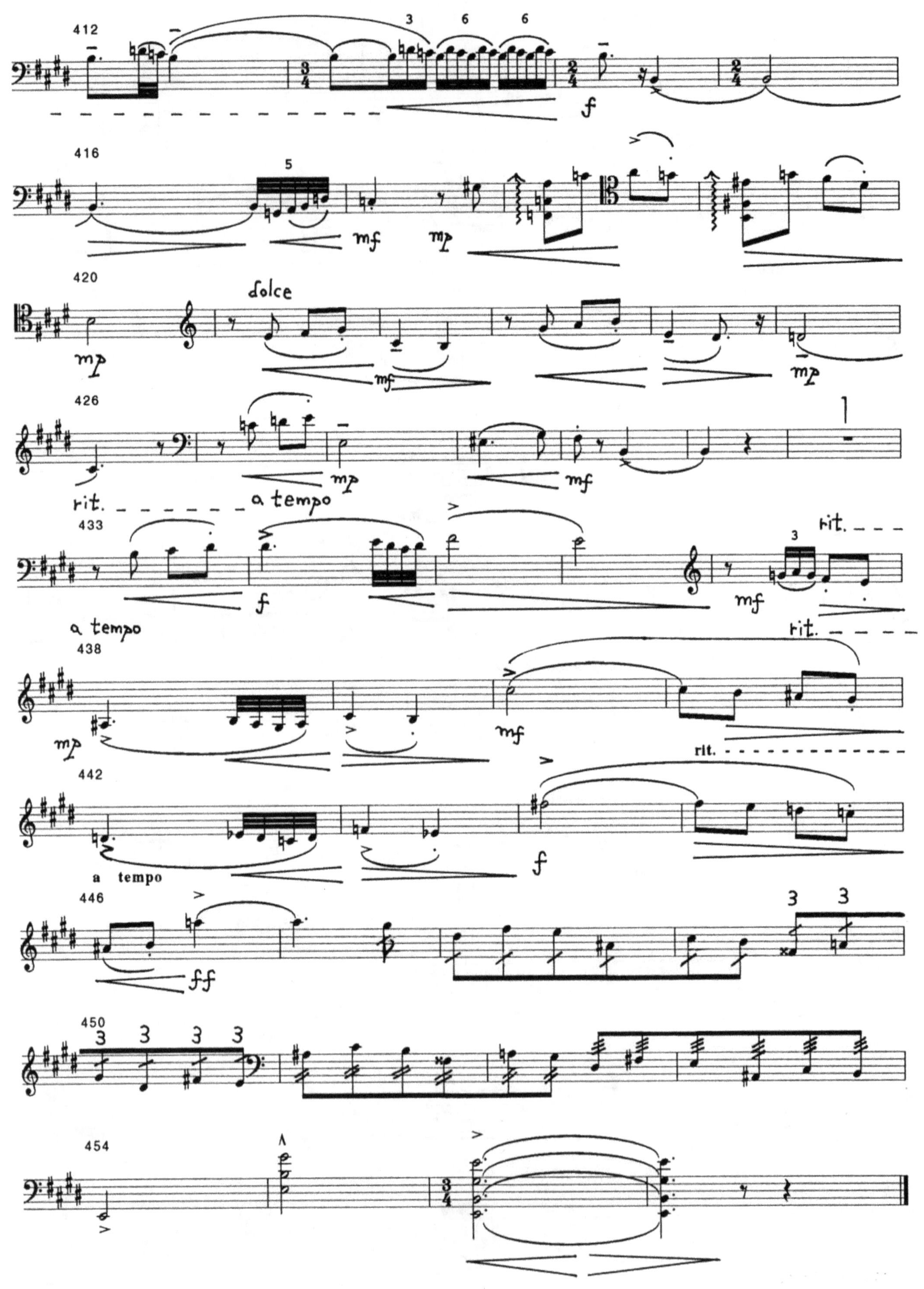
412
f
416
mf
mp
420
mp
dolce
mf
mp
426
rit.
mp
mf
a tempo
433
f
rit.
mf
a tempo
438
mp
mf
rit.
442
a tempo
f
rit.
446
ff
450
454

Fugue in G major
for String Quartet
by Gary Noland
Opus 13
Freeland Publications

Fugue in G major for string quartet

by Gary Noland

dedicated to Beate Perrey

Opus 13, (composed 1978; revised 1989)

Parts may be ordered from Freeland Publications.

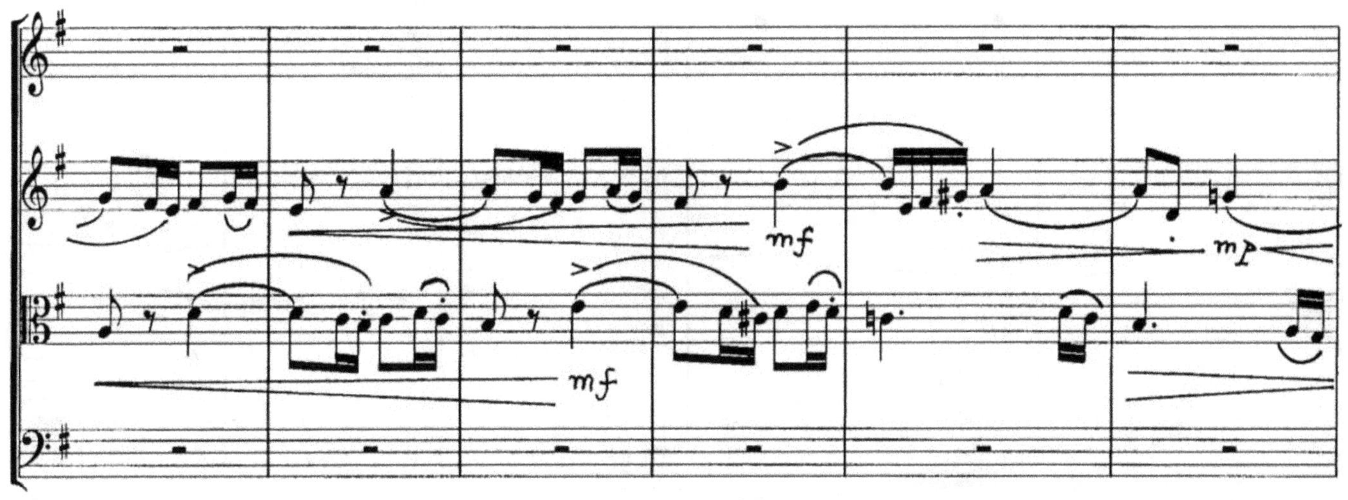
15
mf
mf
mp

20
mf
mp
mp
6

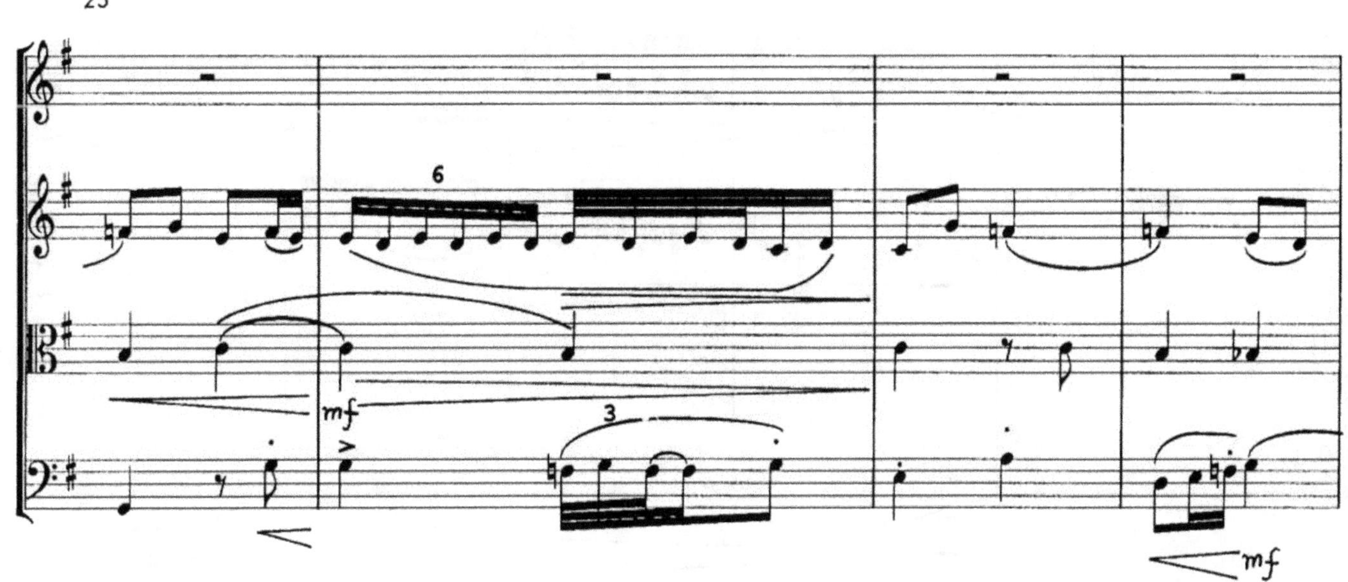
25
6
mf
3
mf

30
mf
6
6
35
40
f
mf
mf

45
50
55
mf
f

60
mp
mp cresc.
mp
cresc.
mp cresc.
65
f
6
f
f
f
6
70
6
6

75
80
85
mf
f

90
mf
mf
mf
mf
95
dim.
dim.
100
mp
mp
mp
mp

Gary Noland
Fugue in G major
for string quartet
Opus 13

Violin I

Freeland Publications

Fugue in G major for string quartet

violin 1

by Gary Noland, Op. 13
(composed 1978; revised 1989)

dedicated to Beate Perrey

74
6
mf
f
79
3
5
mf
f
84
mf
89
96
mp

Gary Noland
Fugue in G major
for string quartet
Opus 13

Violin II

Freeland Publications

Fugue in G major for string quartet

violin 2

dedicated to Beate Perrey

by Gary Noland; Op. 13
(composed 1978; revised 1989)

55
6
mp cresc.
60
f
67
6
73
mf
f
79
mf
f
85
mf
91
dim.
97
mp

Gary Noland
Fugue in G major
for string quartet
Opus 13

Viola

Freeland Publications

Fugue in G major for string quartet

viola

by Gary Noland; Op. 13
(composed 1978; revised 1989)

dedicated to Beate Perrey

54
1
mf
mp
cresc.
61
6
f
67
74
6
80
2
mf
f
mf
87
94
mp

Gary Noland
Fugue in G major
for string quartet
Opus 13

Cello

Freeland Publications

Fugue in G major for string quartet

cello

by Gary Noland; Op. 13
(composed 1978; revised 1989)

dedicated to Beate Perrey

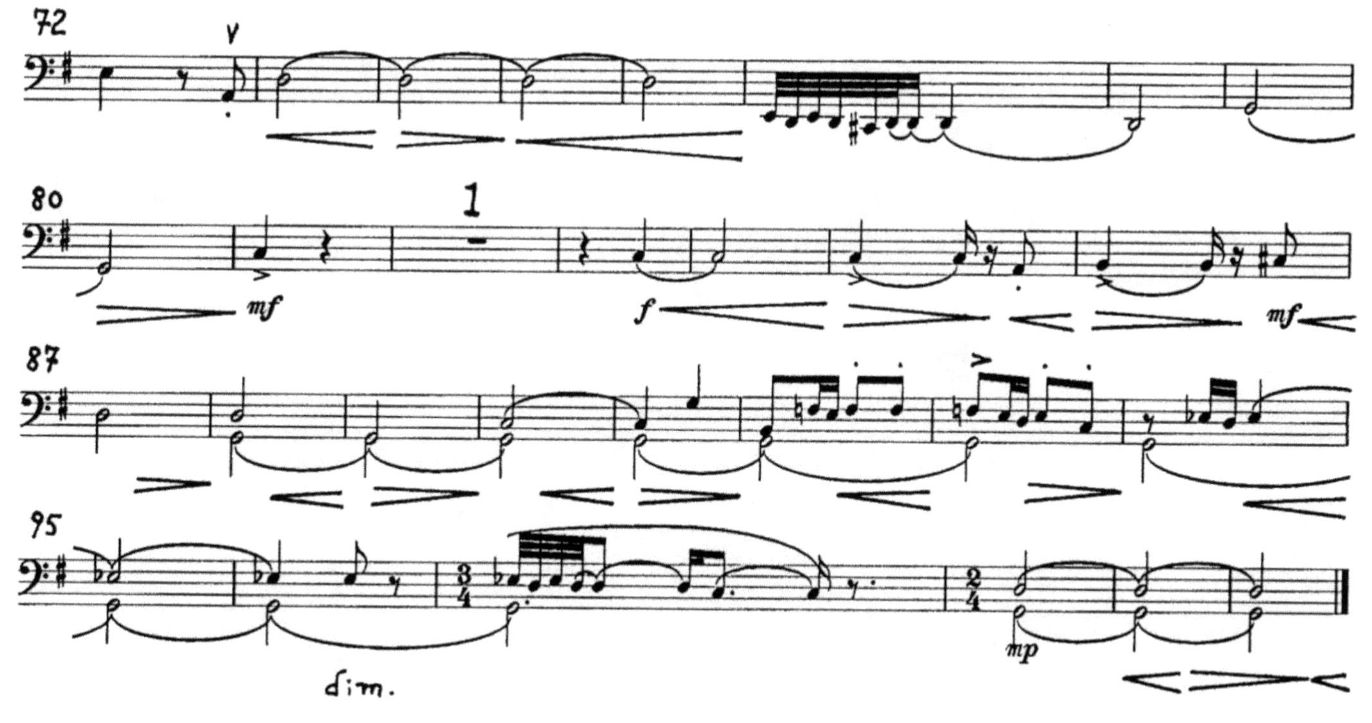
72
80
1
87
95
mf
f
mf
dim.
mp

ABOUT THE COMPOSER

Short Bio (First Person)

I grew up in a headbox as an airhole freak, soliciting gestural acknowledgments of edibility crapropos of my monthly grub. The greenish gruel I ingested for nourishment drizzled in daggers from the broad vicinity of the ropemaster's, the driller's, and the eggman's quarters high aloft in the west-facing sumpwing of my cloaca maxima. I'd wile away my weeks watching ratsnakes swabbling down the dried up, crusty accounts off the edge of the slop pail in which I inveterately soaked my false tooth.

Long Bio (Third Person)

GARY LLOYD NOLAND (a.k.a. author **DOLLY GRAY LANDON**, visual artist **LON GAYLORD DYLAN**, and musicians **ARNOLD DAY LONGLY, ORLAN DOY GLANDLY & DARNOLD OLLY YANG**) was born in Seattle in 1957 and grew up in a broken home in a crowded house shared by ten or more people on a plot of land three blocks south of UC Berkeley known as People's Park, which has distinguished itself as a site of civil unrest since the late 1960s. As an adolescent, Noland lived for a time in Salzburg (Mozart's birthplace) and Garmisch-Partenkirchen (home of Richard Strauss), where he absorbed a host of musical influences. Having studied with a long roster of acclaimed composers and musicians, he earned a Bachelor's degree in music from UC Berkeley in 1979, continued his studies at the Boston Conservatory, and transferred to Harvard University, where he added to his credits a Masters and a PhD in Music Composition in 1989. His teachers in composition and theory have included John Clement Adams (not to be confounded with composers John Coolidge Adams or John Luther Adams), Alan Curtis (harpsichordist, musicologist, conductor, and one of the musical "stars" in Werner Herzog's film on Gesualdo, "Death for Five Voices"), Sir Peter Maxwell Davies (Master of the Queen's Music from 2004-16), William Denny (student of Paul Dukas), Robert Dickow, Janice Giteck (student of Darius Milhaud and Olivier Messiaen), Andrew Imbrie (student of Nadia Boulanger and Roger Sessions, Pulitzer Prize Finalist, 1995), Earl Kim (student of Arnold Schoenberg, Ernest Bloch, and Roger Sessions), Leon Kirchner (student of Arnold Schoenberg and assistant to Ernest Bloch and Roger Sessions, Pulitzer Prize, 1967) David Lewin (dubbed "the most original and far-ranging theorist of his generation"), Donald Martino (student of Milton Babbitt, Roger Sessions, and Luigi Dallapiccola, Pulitzer Prize, 1974), Hugo Norden, Marta Ptaszynska (student of Nadia Boulanger and Olivier Messiaen), Chris Rozé (student of Charles Wuorinen, Ursula Mamlok, and Vincent Persichetti), Goodwin Sammel (student of pianist Claudio Arrau), John Swackhamer (student of Ernst Krenek and Roger Sessions), Ivan Tcherepnin (student of Pierre Boulez and Karlheinz Stockhausen, son of Alexander Tcherepnin), and Walter Winslow (brother of Portland composer Jeff Winslow). Noland has attended seminars by composers David Del Tredici (Pulitzer Prize, 1980), Beverly Grigsby (student of Ernst Krenek), Michael Finnissy (leading British composer and pianist), and Bernard Rands (Pulitzer Prize, 1984), and has had private consultations with George Rochberg ("Father of Neo-Romanticism," Pulitzer Prize finalist, 1986) and Joaquin Nin-Culmell (student of Paul Dukas and Manuel de Falla, brother of essayist and diarist Anaïs Nin).

To continue on with this (undoubtedly tasteless to some) name-dropping pageant, Noland has also had the honor of meeting (howsoever briefly) such luminaries as Lukas Foss (who was highly supportive of him and with whom he maintained a brief correspondence), Elliot Carter, George Crumb, Frederic Rzewski, John Adams, Virgil Thomson, Oswald Jonas (student of Heinrich Schenker, founder of the Schenker Institut), John Corigliano, Stephen Hough, Henry Martin (composer of "WTC III"), Tison Street, Gunther Schuller, John Harbison, Peter Lieberson (five-time Pulitzer Prize finalist and son of the former president of Columbia Records Goddard Lieberson), Lina Prokofiev (wife of Sergei Prokofiev, with whom Noland once had a brief afternoon tête-à-tête), Sir Peter Pears (the English tenor whose career was long associated with that of composer Benjamin Britten), English mezzo-soprano Dame Janet Baker, Alvin Curran, Charles Amirkhanian, Marc-André Hamelin, Gyorgi Ligeti, Hsueh-Yung Shen (composer and percussionist extraordinaire, student of Nadia Boulanger, Darius Milhaud, and Lukas Foss), John Zorn (under whose baton he once performed), Noam Elkies (leading Harvard mathematician and composer), Robert Levin, Tomas Svoboda, and (thru correspondence): Joseph Fennimore, Ladislav Kupkovic, William Bolcom, Max Morath, and others. He also found himself on various occasions within spitting reach of (though didn't quite have the chutzpah at the time to waylay) composers Olivier Messiaen, John Cage, Arvo Pärt, Alfred Schnittke, Hans Werner Henze, William Albright, Brian Ferneyhough, Leslie Bassett, Luciano Berio (next to whom he once sat at a concert), Milton Babbitt, John Williams, Pierre Boulez, John McCabe, and others. In the early 1990's Noland used to dine with a friend of his grandmother's who recounted the story of having once met Gustav Mahler and Bruno Walter while on a hike in the hills outside of Vienna. On the darker side, Noland once met a woman in Cambridge who recounted having attended parties hosted by government officials in Berlin as a young girl in the 1930s where she witnessed her mother (whose husband was an ambassador representing a neutral Latin American country at the time) dancing with none other than (blech!) Adolf Hitler, who had been on friendly terms with descendants of Richard Wagner. Noland's maternal grandparents, who, along with his mother and uncle, fled the Nazis in 1936, recounted how they would often see Einstein (who knew Leopold Godowsky and Arnold Schoenberg) stroll past their home in Berlin back in the 1920s and early 1930s. (*Und so weiter und so fort...*)

One can go on and on recounting other historical connections, interlinkages, and associations Noland has had with famous and important musicians and non-musicians alike. This is not meant in any way, shape, or form to reflect favorably (or, for that matter, unfavorably) upon Noland's own creative endeavors but only as testimony to how privileged he has been (for which he is eternally grateful) to have either met and/or to have been in close proximity to such a legion of distinguished, powerful, and influential luminaries. To those readers who are easily offended by (and/or are inclined to view) this autobiographical account as being blatantly disingenuous and/or self-aggrandizing in tone, the composer offers his semi-sincere condolences for what may, not unforeseeably, smack of shameless name-dropping. One needs must admit, howso, that such shoulder-rubbings as hereinbefore described are highly instructive insofar as shedding light upon the streams of musico-artistic influences that are paramountly important in consideration of how they tend to impact, and ultimately lend cohesion and coherence to, the sum and substance of a composer's creative oeuvre. This is by no means out of the ordinary, for the power of such lineal influences upon artists is empirically universal—they all tend to eat off of one another's plates. There are deep cultural, historical, and psychological explanations (call them "roots" if thou wilt) as to why a composer writes a specific kind of music, and his or her reasons for doing so are less a matter of choice than due to some overpowering inner compulsion over which he or she has only the minutest modicum of self-control. Multiple attempts have been made (by critics and others) to pigeonhole Noland into some pre-defined aesthetic category or school of thought. As a composer, he has often been (mis)labeled as "avant-garde," "neo-romantic," "neo-classical," "modernist," "minimalist," "maximalist,' "postmodern," "radical," "reactionary," "tonal," "atonal," "dadaist," "romantic," "neo-baroque," and/or "iconoclastic" (among other things). None of these tags or isms, in and of themselves, are adequate to describe who he is or what he does (even the charge of iconoclasticism is a bit skewed), and most of these applied logos are not only functionally irrelevant but consummately meaningless. The composer eschews such classifications, since the affixtures of such generic diagnostic labels to one's body of work can prove immensely misleading to an otherwise grossly misinformed public at large. One need only instance what is known as the "Bolero Syndrome" to back up this point, lest there be any bones of contention thereanent, for howsoever adventitious such typecasting may be, it nurtures the inherent potentiality of damnifying a composer's reputability, especially amongst his or her peers of the musical realm. Noland's music has drawn innumberable comparisons (and fomblitudes) to a wide range of compositional influences, including music by composers as sundry and divers as the likes of Richard Strauss, John Cage, Frederic Chopin, Karlheinz Stockhausen, J.S. Bach, Robert Schumann, John Zorn, Max Reger, W. A. Mozart, Olivier Messiaen, Edward Elgar, Franz Schubert, Frederic Rzewski, George Rochberg, Conlon Nancarrow, Frank Zappa, Scott Joplin, Charles Ives, Ludwig van Beethoven, Cecil Taylor, John Dowland, Thelonius Monk, Johannes Brahms, Arnold Schönberg, Phillip Glass, Gustav Mahler, Erik Satie, and many others. A marked preponderance of such similitudinizations rings, perhaps, with occasional discrete elements of truth (and is, nevertheless, not unflattering to the recipient thereof, as such comparisons can in most cases be taken as encomiums) but none of these things even marginally suffice to tell the story of who the composer is, what his most matterable and momentous accomplishments are, why he writes the kind of music he does, or what his compositions signify in connection with the historical context(s) in which they are produced.

One can only hope against all hopes that, in virtue of the all-pervasive corruption and depravity distinguishing the bureaucrappic abomination that, until only a few short months ago (at the time of this writing), wielded its rubber fists unrelentingly over the politico-moral ideologies of the swank-and-vile for the purpose of breeding a veritable death cult inwith the bottommost echelons of its schlubordinate ranks (namely: those who would, according to its pre-calculatory caballings, be totalitarianly rightwashed into obsequiously serving not just the baby-fingered monster's pecuniary but also its hell-fired ego-bloating exigencies), as betwixt and betweentimes it empowers, and therewith imbibulates, its fetid effluvium to permeate each and every constituent element of the existing sociocultural milieu—Dandies & Gentledames: welcome to the COVID era!—'twould in a slump be perceived, by those possessing even the paltriest iota of hypo-critical acumen, as a perfectly natural outcome of the ubiquitous surfeit of ignormation and improperganda coupled with the complexity of kinks and viewpoints that have evolved as a result of the chaotic musical landscape that has emerged in recent quinquennia (not to fight shy of unmentioning the multiplicity of dinfluences, once accessible only to the topmost echelons of the eggheaded elite, that has been globally disseminated by dint of an ultroneous cross-pollination of diverse and powerful artistic lineages, as well as the commingling and interfusing of snub-cultures, past and present alike), which may well serve to impact, and ultimately lend a sort of structural cohesion (assuming that such a phenomenon is not pre-indisposed to be steemed a desirable asset inwith the prevailing ethico-moral codes of the present frivolizational ethos) to an artist's creative output (presupposing overmore that the artist under scrutiny is a thinking individual who has achieved a markedly eminent plateau of craftsmanly adroitness), that one's critical response thereto would, at an irreducible minimum, be that of paying a fitting tribute (insofar as putting one's celery where one's mouth is, that is) by granting formal agnition (even though in all likelihood "too-little-toolate," having been mongo decenniums overdue) to the creative outpourings (whether willful on the part of the perpetrator or no) as being LEGIT, AUTHENTIC and/or preeminently AUTHORITATIVE works of artistic expression.

To polemicize, hammergag, or stupinionate obstreperously to the contrary—that is, insofar as afforcing to delegitimize the brainchildren of unexceptionably accomplished creators by virtue of the convenient dismission of their effections in the vein of stigmatizing them for manifesting uncorroborated mouthprints of "derivativeness," "historicism," "pastiche" and suchlike (hackneyed forms of faultfinding, accidentarily, that have in due season come to represent the stereotypical tropes that have, time out of number, been shown to possess an instinctible propensity for oozing their way diarrhoeically from the hollowed, sphinct-like groves of vainstream cacademe, and the formalistically run-of-the-drill, accreditated musics of which have also not unfailed to disprove, over and again, to have scarce if any shelf-life in the unadulterated domain of contemporary classical ear-meat manufacturing)—would be either disingenuous, naïve, or dazzlingly indolent on the part of the criticasters under scrutiny.

Far offshore as it might seem, it has come to this dotmaker's attention, thru empirical observations conducted over a quaternity of decades, that 'tis often-whiles not unprone to be the case that the more refined, facete, and scrupulously rigorous the caliber of the craftsmanship and artistry of a given musical production is fair to be—and one oughtn't make any bones about the effect that stylistic distinctiveness per se is all but impossimaginable without a composer achieving a consummate mastery of his or her art (a truism powered by ample historical evidence)—the more probable it is that charges of "pastiche" and other opprobrious, derogatory abusions will be leveled against said composer by invidious flubdubs, ableless wannabes, affectatious morons, conceited simpletons, pompous nincompoops, impenitent philistines, and ladders of other insufferably bombastic socialclimbing snoots, parasites, toadies, and other bottom-feeding intestinal cack-weasels, microbes, barnacles, maggots, and the like. There is no "straight and narrow" in the art of music creation—it is an indescribably messy and chaotic affair that necessitates a fierce, sustained, and uncompromising focus of fanatically devoted attention and feverish concentration, never mind a preternatural willingness to have the mockers put on one's dignity and through-bearing, even to the point, perforce, of dicing with one's very own death. One of Noland's self-coined aphorisms is: "There are no rules in love, war, and art." Another, based upon an inversion of filmmaker Luis Buñuel's celebrious quism, reads: "Art without craft is like salt without an egg."

Gary Lloyd Noland's ever-expanding catalogue consists of scores of opuses, which include piano, vocal, chamber, orchestral, experimental, and electronic pieces, full-length plays in verse, "chamber novels," and graphically notated scores. His critically acclaimed, award-winning 77-hour long *Gesamtkunstwerk* JAGDLIED: a Chamber Novel for Narrator, Musicians, Pantomimists, Dancers & Culinary Artists (Op. 20) was listed by one reviewer as the Number

One book of 2018. His "39 Variations on an Original Theme in F Major" for solo piano Op. 98 (included in this collection) is, at approximately two hours duration, one of the lengthiest and most challenging sets of solo piano variations in the history of the genre. It has been called by American composer Ernesto Ferreri "an historical variation set for piano, a true descendant of the Goldbergs and Diabellis, beautifully targeted to an apotheosis of supreme grandeur." Composer/pianist Ludwig Tuman described it as "an astounding tour de force. In its far-reaching, systematic exploration of the theme's creative possibilities, as well as in the inexhaustible imagination brought to bear, it reminds one of the Goldberg and the Diabelli. But in its monumental dimensions it goes far beyond them both, and in the large number of historical styles referenced and integrated into the work … I am unaware of any parallel. I especially enjoyed the consistent use of certain features of the theme, regardless of the style or the type of tonality, pantonality or atonality employed—among them the melodic turn, the phrases ascending by whole steps, and others. I offer my humble congratulations on a titanic achievement!"

Having received both effusive praise and violent censure of his music over the years, Noland has been called "the Richard Strauss of the 21st century," "the [Max] Reger of the 21st century," "the most prominent American composer (of modern classical music) of our times," "the most virtuosic composer of fugue alive today," "the composer to end all composers," "court jester to the classical establishment," and "one of the great composers of the 21st century," and has on numerous occasions been branded a "genius." He has also been called some pretty colorful names by his detractors—names unsuitable for publication in the pages of this volume. Although the composer feels something of a constitutional disinclination to share with his prospective groupies the aforesaid hyperbolical quotations, as it causes him (howsoever unwittingly) to mount a red flag, he is clevertheless all but compelled to trumpet such encomiums for the sake of ensuring his survival in the present-day blaringly obnoxious, braggadocious milieu, notwithgrandstanding that he is neither flannelmouthed nor overweening by nature but—quite *au contraire*—of a singularly equanimous poise and disposition. Unfreely farouche and retiring by nature, composer Noland is, by his own admission (and, beyond peradventure, to his ultimate detriment) an ineradicably head-in-the-clouds introvert par *excellence*.

Noland's compositions have been performed and broadcast (including on NPR) in many locations throughout the United States, as well as in Europe, Asia, and Australia. His music has also been heard on six continents via various music-streaming platforms. Noland founded the Seventh Species Contemporary Classical Music Concert Series in San Francisco in 1990 and has, since, produced upwards of fifty-plus concerts of contemporary classical music on the West Coast. He is also a founding member of Cascadia Composers, which has, since the time of its inception in 2008, mushroomed into a veritable colossus of an organization supporting regional and national composers, as well as performers of contemporary classical music, and has, furtherover, distinguished itself as one of the premier collectives of its kind on the West Coast. Noland has taught music at Harvard, the University of Oregon, and a couple of community colleges (bleah!), and currently teaches piano, theory, and composition as a private independent instructor in the Portland, Oregon metro area.

A number of Noland's works (fiction, music, and graphic scores) have been published (and/or are slated for publication) in various litmags, including Quarter After Eight, Berkeley Fiction Review, Portland Review, Denali, The Monarch Review, Prick of the Spindle, theNewerYork Press, Wisconsin Review, The Writing Disorder, and Heavy Feather Review. His graphic scores are included in Theresa Sauer's book NOTATIONS 21 (2009), which is a sequel to John Cage's celebrated compilation of graphic scores: NOTATIONS (first published in 1969). A chapter on Noland is included in Burl Willes's celebrated book TALES FROM THE ELMWOOD: A COMMUNITY MEMORY published by the Berkeley Historical Society in 2000. In 1999 Noland was awarded the Oregon Composer of the Year Award jointly by the Oregon Music Teachers Association (OMTA) and Music Teachers National Association (MTNA) and was commissioned to compose his SEPTET for clarinet, saxophone, French horn, two violins, double bass, and piano (Op. 43). Noland's GRANDE RAG BRILLANTE Op. 15 (included in this collection) was commissioned by KPFA Radio to celebrate the inauguration of its (then, in 1991) brand new Pacifica Radio Headquarters in Berkeley. This premiere was later acknowledged in Nicolas Slonimsky's book MUSIC SINCE 1900.

Many of Noland's scores are available from J.W. Pepper, RGM, Sheet Music Plus, and Freeland Publications. Six CDs of his compositions are available on the North Pacific Music label at northpacificmusic.com. Nine more new CDs of his compositions will be made available in the near future. Over 400 videos and audio recordings of Noland's music and narratives are available for listening and viewing on YouTube, Vimeo, Soundcloud, Spotify, Apple Music, Amazon Music, Pandora and hosts of other music streaming networks worldwide. Most of Noland's music videos and audio recordings are also available for viewing and listening on his website: http://www.composergarynoland.godaddysites.com/

Noland's COLLECTED PIANO WORKS: Volume 1 is available for purchase at many major book retailers worldwide. Here is the Amazon link at which it can be ordered: https://www.amazon.com/Collected-Piano-Works-Lloyd-Noland/dp/1732302383/ref=asc_df_1732302383/?tag=hyprod-20&linkCode=df0&hvadid=539702681678&hvpos=&hvnetw=g&hvrand=1583536589030730437 4&hvpone=&hvptwo=&hvqmt=&hvdev=c&hvdvcmdl=&hvlocint=&hvlocphy=9032854&hvtargid=pla-1412571247136&psc=1

Noland's award-winning chamber novel JAGDLIED is currently available for purchase at: https:// www.amazon.com/gp/product/B07GJ1RDQJ?pf_rd_p=183f5289-9dc0-416f-942e-e8f213ef368b&pf_rd_r=FJW5GVTYY1NKTJ47M5B5

Noland's critically acclaimed six-hour play NOTHING IS MORE: A HIGH BLACK COMEDY IN VERSE WITH MUSIC FOR SIX ACTORS is available for purchase at: https://www.amazon.com/Nothing-More-Black-Comedy-Actors/dp/1795387513/ref=tmm_pap_swatch_0?_encodi

Also available from 7th Species Publications

Gary Lloyd Noland's COLLECTED PIANO WORKS: Volumes 1 and 2, which can be ordered from most major, and many independent, book retailers worldwide, including Amazon, Target, Walmart, Powell's Books, Discover Books, and many others. These eminently affordable 286-page volumes offer multi-faceted compilations of Noland's compositions for piano spanning the last three decades of the 20th century to the present (2021). The pieces included in these collections range in level from lower intermediate to upper advanced.

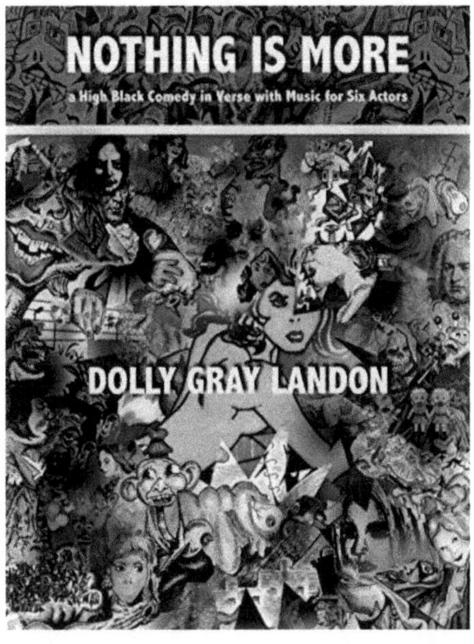

Authored under an anagrammatic version of the composer's name, which he uses as his author pen name, Dolly Gray Landon's (née Gary Lloyd Noland's) subversively hilarious six-hour play NOTHING IS MORE is a high black comedy in doggerel verse with music for six fiercely opinionated and outspoken characters with radically different perverspectives apropos of what constitutes "art," ranging from the commercially pragmatic to the philosophically effete. The opinions expressed are in no ways frivolous but evolve into transcendental matters verging on Life and Death. The setting is Pimpleton State Luniversity, which offers a post-doctoral degree called a "stool" for scholars specializing in absurdly arcane areas of research (e.g., Primaeval Linguistics, Feline Transgender Studies, Astromusicology). Amongst the stool program's leading contenders is a bombastically pretentious charlatan named Phangbang Bonation, who is the prolific progenitor of a post-postmodernist aesthetic known as "Nadaism," which espouses the submicrominimalist credo that producing zilch (i.e., nothing at all) is a legitimate form of artistic expression. This deranged ideology draws a huge cult following amongst critics of all artistic genres and earns Phangbang untold wealth in the sales (thru auctions) of various non-opuses from his Nadaistic oeuvre. Two of his fellow stool candidates—Pelvin Penisovich and Purvel Schlignatz—are so violently repelled by Phangbang's grandiose pretensions (especially subsequent to his diverting the amorous attentions of their main squeezes exclusively to himself), that they spare no effort in forging an elaborate scheme to expose him for the cunning impostor they adamantly believe him to be in the hopes of not only irrevocably invalidating him and his cockamamie ideas about art but also of obliterating him and his Nadaistic movement from the face of the earth. Notwithstanding the foregoing, nothing turns out the way Pelvin and Purvel envisioned it ought to have subsequent to carrying out their nefarious enterprise, as they learn, to their utmost dismay, that they have unwittingly opened a whole new (and even more appalling) Pandora's box of depraved theoretical dogmas as to what constitutes an authentic form of creative expression. Thus, their foiled attempt to subvert what they perceive as the unholy aesthetic crusade of their rodomont adversary ends up backfiring upon them in the form of a new post-postmodernist school of thought that blindly enthused critics coin as "revisitationism," which engenders in its turn the unleashing of a plague of criticastically acclaimed, up-to-the-minute, pseudo-artistic horrorshows all across the land. The following caveat should not be construed as a spoiler alert but rather as a friendly heads-up to prospective explorers of this text. Readers and audients are duly advised of the very palpable likelihood that they will be rendered speechless—even dumb—when they find out what the aforementioned revolutionary artistic innovation embodies. Be forewarned: This play is not intended for weak-kneed invertebrates or the squeamish of heart.